Scales Bootcamp

ISBN 978-0-9581905-4-1
ver. 2.0

Philip's YouTube Channel:
Search for "Philip Johnston piano" at YouTube.

Also by Philip Johnston

Not Until You've Done Your Practice (1989)

The Practice Revolution (2002)

Practiceopedia (2007)

The Dynamic Studio (2012)

Rhythm Bootcamp (2014)

Bootcamp Editions (2015-)

insidemusicteaching.com

thebootcampedition.com

Welcome to

Helping you figure out new scales quickly

No other scales manual gets you up and running so fast. The graphical keyboard reference in *Scales Bootcamp* has each new scale leaping off the page, all secrets laid bare. There's nothing to figure out; just play what you see.

Helping you master scales, so you know them for life

As surely as you know the alphabet, your times tables, your birthday. To get you there, we've borrowed from computer game design, stolen from *Practiceopedia* (see the "Boot Camp" entry), and packed this book with Challenges to complete for each new scale, giving your scales practice a *purpose*.

Fanatical attention to the scales you'll actually use

Instead of being a museum of every scale ever invented, *Scales Bootcamp* is about getting you very, very good at the scales you'll work with most often. Majors, harmonic minors and chromatics, taken through the most rigorous combination of drills and challenges, all leading to an extraordinary promise…

…tick every box for a scale, you'll know it for life

Whether you ever practice it again, or not (!)

Of course, *ticking every box* means you will have practiced the scale every which way, and then some...that's the whole point. Nothing prepares you like Bootcamp.

Bootcamp

Before you start #1: Core groups

Unlike most scales manuals, *Scales Bootcamp* shows all notes and fingerings on keyboards. This is so you can instantly see what to play, which fingers to use.

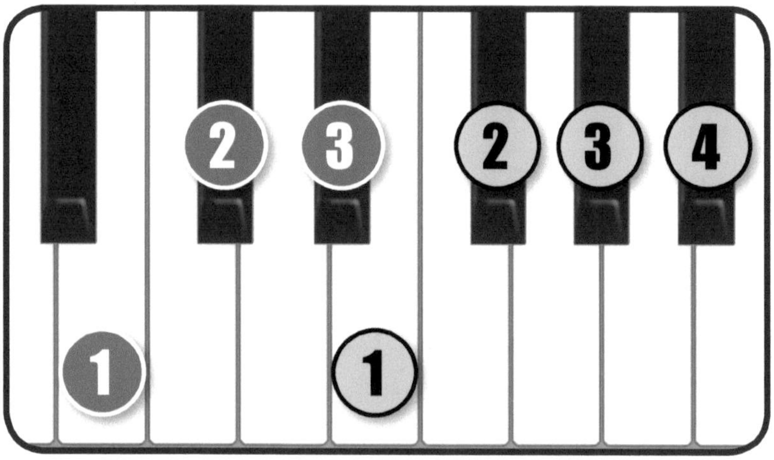

Red circles show groups of **1-2-3***

* 3-2-1 in Left Hand

Blue circles show groups of **1-2-3-4***

* 4-3-2-1 in Left Hand

This book uses color coding to highlight all groups of 1-2-3 and 1-2-3-4, because—and it comes as a shock to many pianists—*all your scales are built from alternating groups of 1-2-3 and 1-2-3-4.*

The fastest way to learn a new scale—and the most secure way to remember it—is not to try to memorize long sequences of finger numbers. It's to know where these **groups** of 1-2-3 and 1-2-3-4 are.

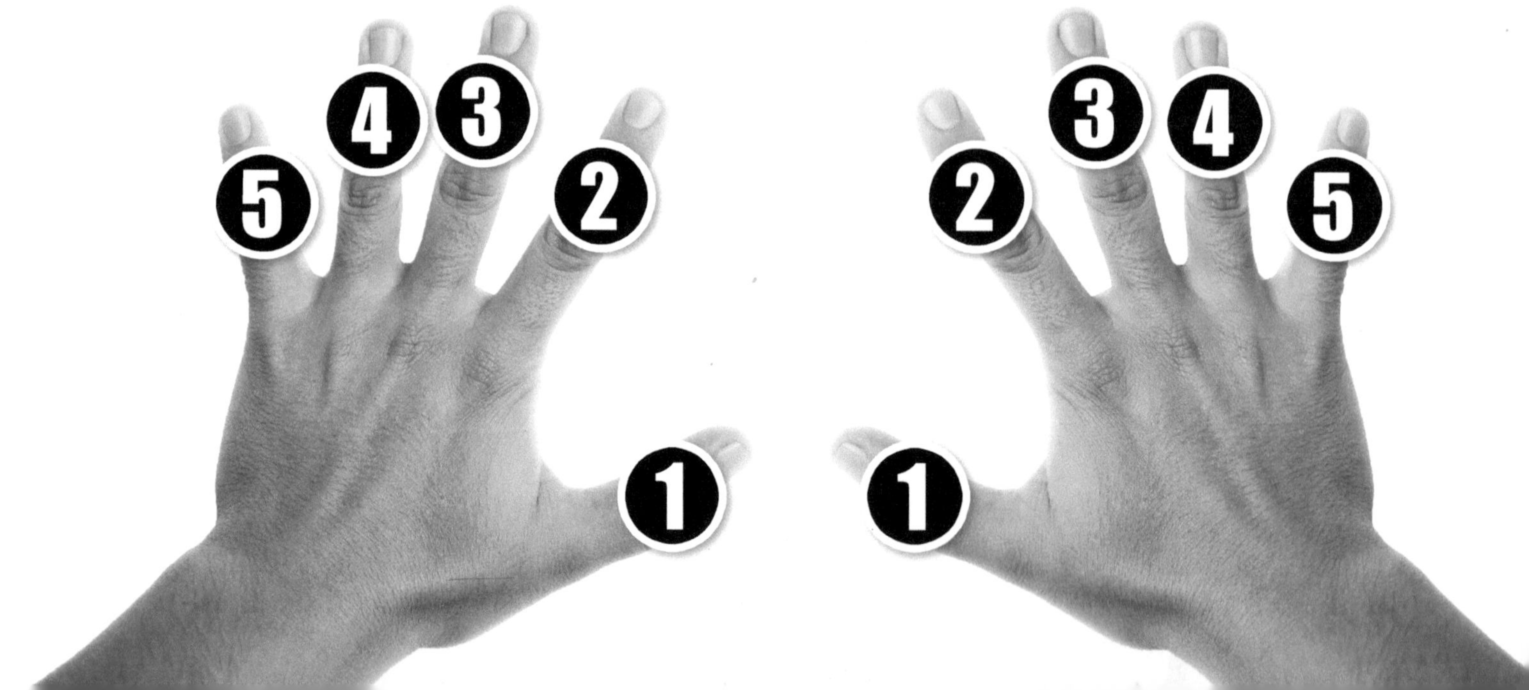

Before you start #1: Core groups

You can see this color coding in the three scales below.
Remember, don't try to memorize individual finger numbers.
Instead, look for groups of 1-2-3 and 1-2-3-4.

A Major, Right Hand

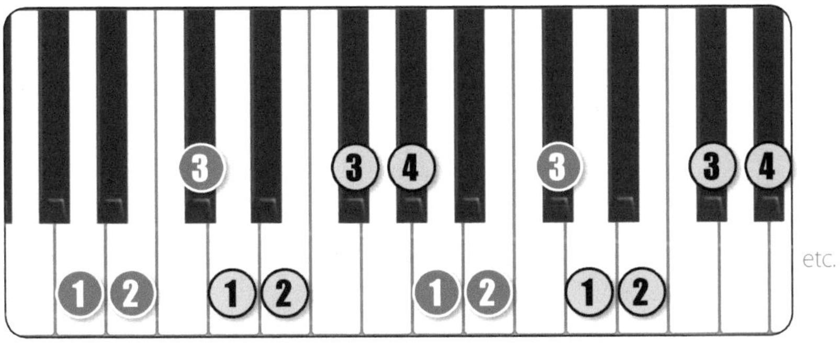

C# Minor, Left Hand (order is reversed for left hand)

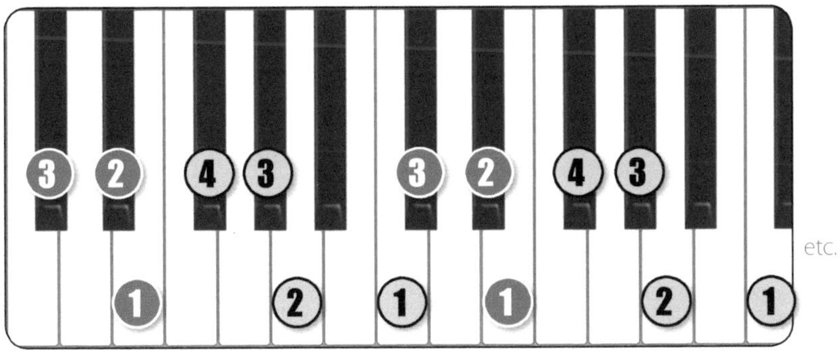

E Minor, Right Hand

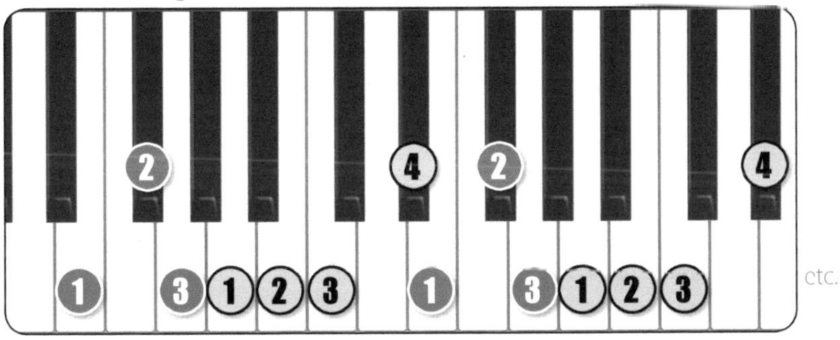

Notice how the color-coding makes the 1-2-3 and 1-2-3-4 groups stand out; in fact, **even if there were no finger numbers** marked at all, you'd quickly be able to figure out what to use…

Before you start #1: Core groups

. . .try it for yourself. We've removed all fingering from this **right hand** scale; use the color-coding and see if you can figure out what should be there:

(See page 35 for the answer)

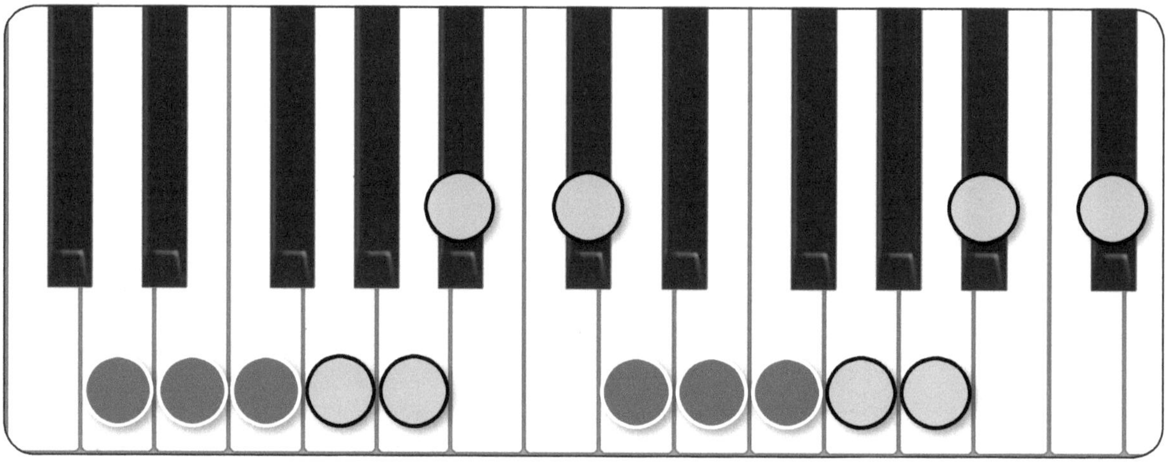

...or this scale for the **left Hand** (note: *Left* hand, so each group is reversed—instead of blue indicating 1-2-3-4, use 4-3-2-1—but it's exactly the same idea.)

(See page 50 for the answer)

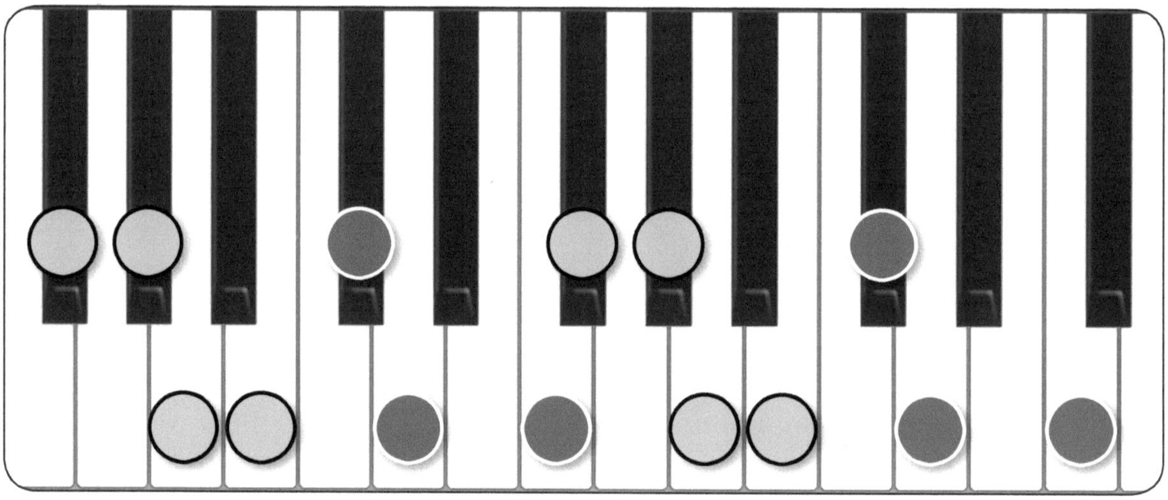

There's plenty of fingering in *Scales Bootcamp*, but really, you won't need most of it. The color-coding does 98% of the heavy lifting for you.

Before you start #2: Bookends

All these red and blue groups make life much easier, but there is an exception to watch out for. Some scales **start** or **end** with a special fingering that doesn't belong to a 1-2-3 or 1-2-3-4 group. Whenever this happens, that "bookend" fingering is shown in a black circle.

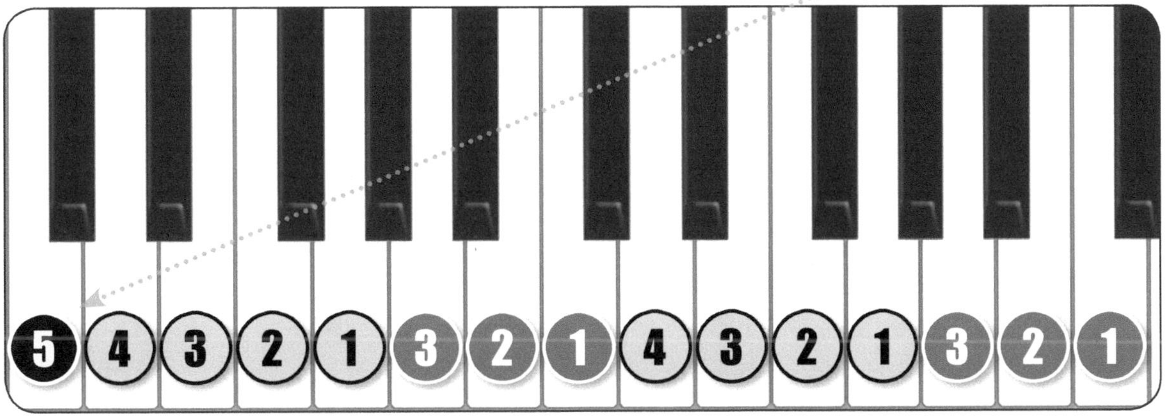

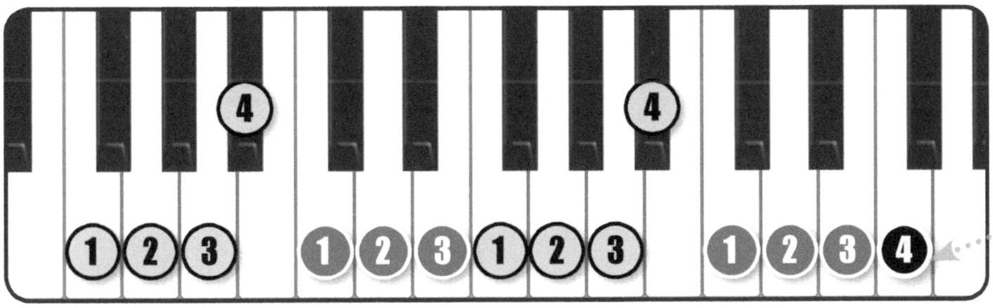

Here's an example of a bookend at the **end** of a scale.

You'll also sometimes see bookends with **more than one note** in them:

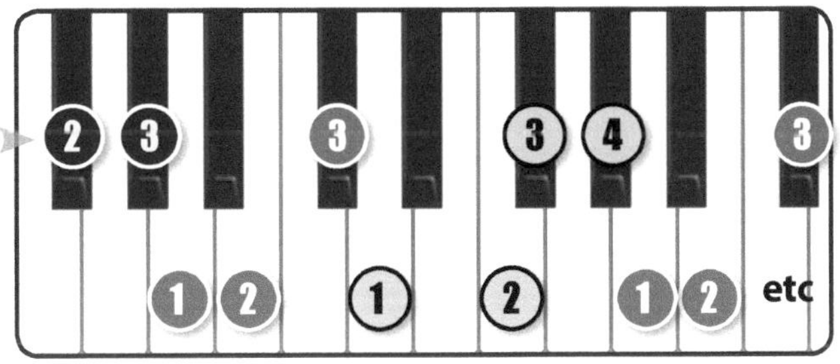

Bookends are common. Most of the major and minor scales in this book feature bookends.

You won't find a *set* of bookends in the same scale for the same hand. So if you're playing separate hands, a bookend will either be at the top, ***or*** the bottom of the scale, but never both.

Notice though that apart from the bookends themselves, the rest of the scale is **still groups of 1-2-3 and 1-2-3-4.**

Before you start #3: Ghosts

The only other wrinkle is that sometimes a group of 1-2-3 or 1-2-3-4 doesn't appear in full—simply because the scale **runs out of notes** before the group can be completed.Take a look at the right hand of F# Major:

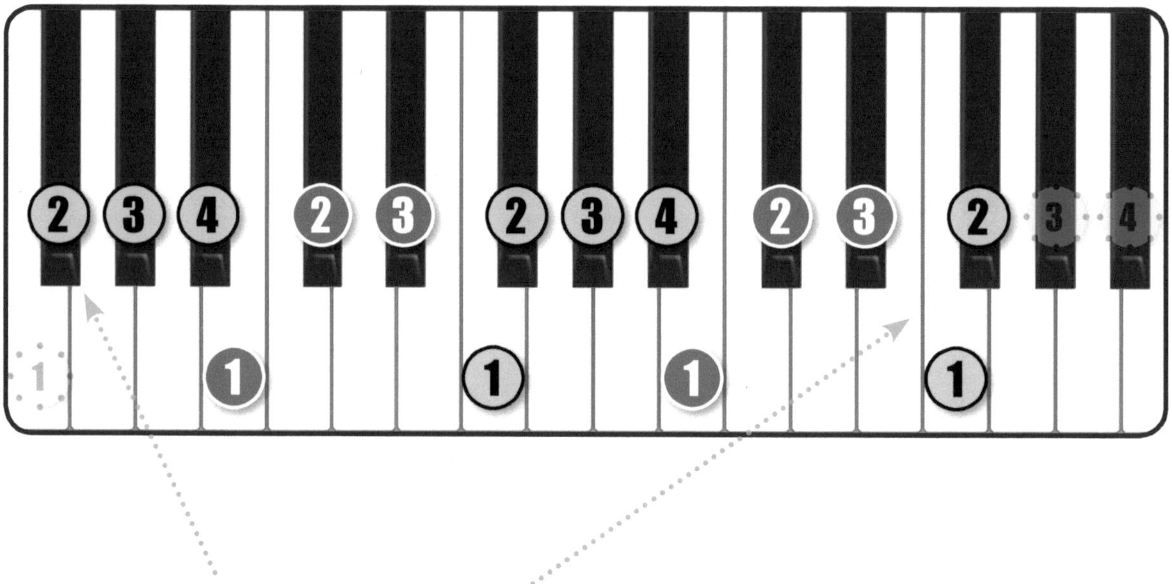

This scale is still 1-2-3-4 alternating with 1-2-3...it's just that at the bottom and top of the scale, the 1-2-3-4 group starts or ends midway through.

The **ghosted notes** show what *would* have happened, had the scale continued. If you picture those ghosted notes (but don't play them), you'll easily be able to work out what finger the scale starts or ends on.

Before you start #3: Ghosts

Here's **another example of ghost notes.** Again—like all your scales—this C# Major scale is built from groups of 1-2-3 alternating with groups of 1-2-3-4...

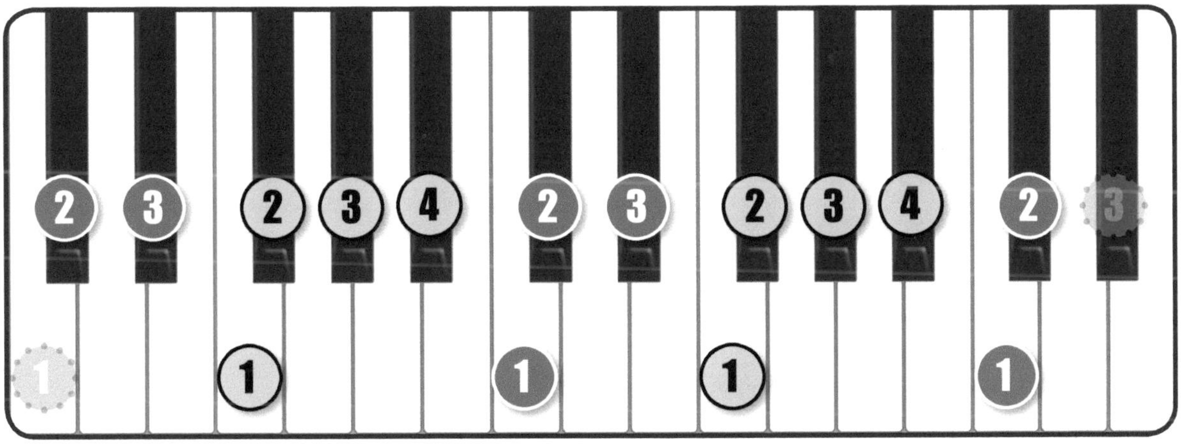

Unlike bookends (see Page 7)—*which are the only irregularities in your scales*—it's important to think of ghosts as just being part of the regular 1-2-3, 1-2-3-4 fingering pattern.

(We've color coded them as if they were part of regular groups, so that you *will* think of them that way).

Fun facts about ghost notes

- **Only 8** of the scales in this book feature ghost notes.
- You'll only find ghosts in scales that **start on black notes.**
- **Like bookends**, ghosts only ever appear at the very top or very bottom of a scale. **Unlike bookends** though, ghosts can appear at both the bottom *and* the top of the same scale in the same hand.
- Any scale that does not have a bookend will **definitely have ghosts!**

Before you start #4: FAQs

I've met my new scale. How do I *master* it though?

At the bottom of each scale's page, there is a huge collection of Challenges to complete; almost 200 for each scale, in fact.

By the time you've ticked just half the boxes in that list, you'll be very, very good at your new scale. Tick *all* of them, and we promise, the scale will be yours for life.

Are you serious about the "Yours for Life" promise?

Absolutely. You may *choose* to work on the scale again—you can always makes scales more legato, or strive for a more beautiful tone—but you won't ever need to revise the scale again to stay familiar with the notes and fingerings. Like your teacher, you'll just *know* them.

How do I know what each Challenge requires?

68

The boxed page number next to each Challenge will point you to page number of the instructions you need. The Challenges have been designed to be easy to understand...not always so easy to actually *complete* though ☺

Do I have to complete the Challenges in order?

No, there's no rule like that—you can tackle Challenges in any order you like. You could earn the Left Hand (LH) Challenge tick for one scale, and then the RH tick for a different Challenge for an entirely different scale...the route you take through *Scales Bootcamp* is up to you.

What are scales "twists"?

These are special Challenges that will really test your command of the scale (and your sanity). Expect huge variations in rhythms, articulations, dynamics and much more...just like you'll experience when scales appear in your actual repertoire.

If there is *anything* at all about the scale that you're not sure of, you'll overload, and the scale will crash—there's just too much else to think about for you to fake your way through Twists. See the back of the book for the full collection.

What is meant by "Levelling up?"

It's similar to what happens in a lot of computer games. Complete enough Challenges, and your scale will qualify for a new rank. So, for example, as soon as you've completed any 8 Challenges, your scale rank is promoted to "Apprentice". To be promoted to "Experienced, you'd need 19 more Challenges on top of that. To qualify for the top ranking though, you'll need a tick for *every* Challenge.

You'll be able to use these rankings to quickly see where every scale is up to—they can also be handy for studio scales competitions and leaderboards.

Before you start #4: FAQs

How were the color coded difficulty ratings worked out?

Any rating like this will generate plenty of debate, but for the record, we took into account the following:

- The presence of **bookend** or **incomplete** fingerings (or both);
- **Visual complexity** of the scale (do patterns jump out when you first see the scale? Or does the at-a-glance arrangement of black and white notes seem chaotic?);
- How well the scale **fits under the hand** (does the piano almost seemed designed especially for that scale, like B Major? Or does the layout make playing accurately difficult, like B^b minor?);
- To what extent is the Left Hand a **mirror image** of the right hand (both in terms of fingering and layout...the closer the match, the easier to learn both hands);
- What percentage of your **studied repertoire** is likely to have been in this key;
- And the **x factor** (a subjective rating based on my own 20+ years of teaching and watching students wrestle with scales...which scales seemed to cause the most grief?)

Whoa!...some of these Challenges are tough...

They're meant to be tough. Just like boss levels in computer games, be ready for the fact that you'll need to attempt some of these Challenges many, many times before you eventually earn the tick.

But aren't all those repeated attempts really just a type of...

...practice? Well, how about that. ☺

Remember though, because the Challenges and Twists are so varied, your practice will be too. The core of Scales Bootcamp is still plenty of repetition. . .but you won't notice most of it, because you'll be too busy earning Challenge ticks, and trying to get your head around whatever the next Twist is.

That's sneaky.

Thank you.

It's not fair though...in order to earn all the Challenges, I have to be able to play one hand louder than the other/ deliver tricky rhythms with precision/show excellent dynamic control/increase the speed of my playing...

Yes.

So I'm working on much more than just scales here?

It's what scales practice *should* be. Instead of just playing your scales up and down and back again, you're relating them to the sort of challenges that actual repertoire will throw at you. You're also working directly on skills that you need for *all* your playing.

Before you start #4: FAQs

Can my teacher and I make changes to the Bootcamp quest requirements?*

Of course—as long as your teacher agrees. You can make individual quests harder, or easier; you can also change the number of quests required for each Levelling up. The only exception is that the "Yours For Life" Level requires every quest, as is.

(With thanks to Marissa, an 11-year old student user of Rhythm Bootcamp whose email to me inspired this permission)

Sometimes I'm so busy thinking about the Twist or Challenge requirements *that I can't supervise the scale itself...*

...which means that the scale has to be able to run on autopilot. To all but play itself, without you having to think about notes or fingering, while you focus instead on controlling your articulation, your dynamics, your phrasing, your rhythmic precision, balance between hands...

...that's *mastery*. That's the Bootcamp promise.

I'm also wondering if—

—shhh. Enough questions now.
It's time to train.

Bootcamp Index

"...finish all the Challenges for any scale, and you'll know that scale for life*"

*whether you practice it again or not!

Very Easy | Easy | Moderate | Challenging | Difficult

A Minor

Very Easy | Easy | Moderate | Challenging | Difficult

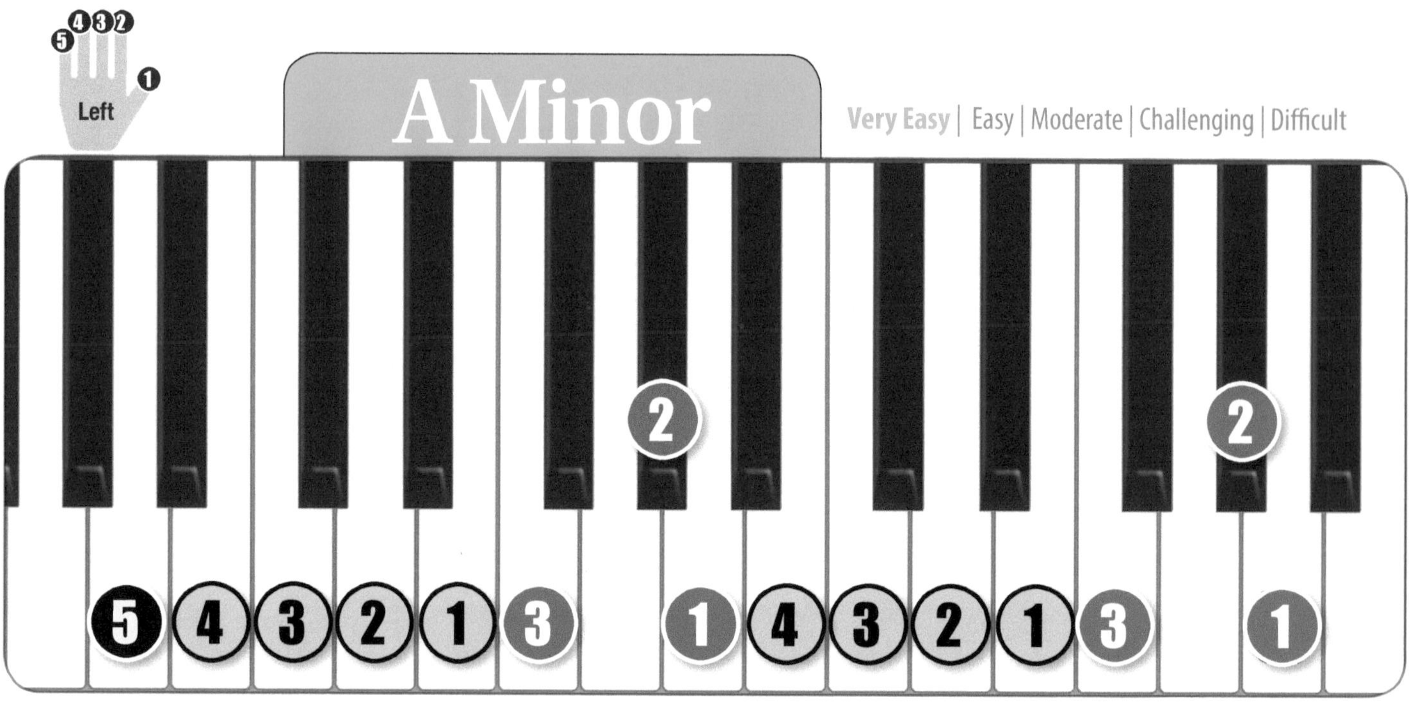

① Core Challenges

Start with these

Page		L	R	T
68	First Playthrough	☐	☐	☐
68	First from Memory	☐	☐	☐
68	First Contrary Motion	–	–	☐
68	4 Octave Tour	☐	☐	☐
69	Grand Tour	☐	☐	☐
69	Thrice is Nice	☐	☐	☐
69	10 in a Row	☐	☐	☐
69	3 Minute Quota	☐	☐	☐
70	3 Minute Tightrope	☐	☐	☐
70	Marathon Tightrope	☐	☐	☐
70	Witnessed by 6	☐	☐	☐
70	Lesson Startup	☐	☐	☐
71	Super Slow Motion	☐	☐	☐
71	Commentator	☐	☐	–
71	Splatmaster	☐	☐	–
72	By Feel Alone	☐	☐	☐
72	Tabletop Scale	☐	☐	☐
72	Repertoire	–	–	☐
72	Octave Collector	☐	☐	☐

L is Left Hand, **R** is Right Hand, **T** is Together

② Tempo Milestones

Gradually speeding it up

Metronome Setting	L	R	T	CM
♩=100 1 note per beat	☐	☐	☐	☐
♩=120 1 note per beat	☐	☐	☐	☐
♩=150 1 note per beat	☐	☐	☐	☐
♩=90 2 notes per beat	☐	☐	☐	☐
♩=105 2 notes per beat	☐	☐	☐	☐
♩=120 2 notes per beat	☐	☐	☐	☐
♩=135 2 notes per beat	☐	☐	☐	☐
♩=150 2 notes per beat	☐	☐	☐	☐
♩=80 4 notes per beat	☐	☐	☐	☐
♩=90 4 notes per beat	☐	☐	☐	☐
♩=100 4 notes per beat	☐	☐	☐	☐
♩=110 4 notes per beat	☐	☐	☐	☐
♩=120 4 notes per beat	☐	☐	☐	☐
♩=130 4 notes per beat	☐	☐	☐	☐
♩=140 4 notes per beat	☐	☐	☐	☐

CM is contrary motion. Contrary scales are 2 octaves, all others are 4 octaves. Must be **twice in a row correct**.

Very Easy | Easy | Moderate | Challenging | Difficult

A Minor

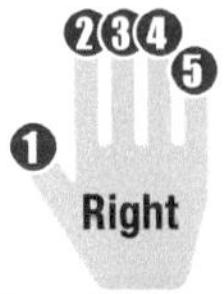

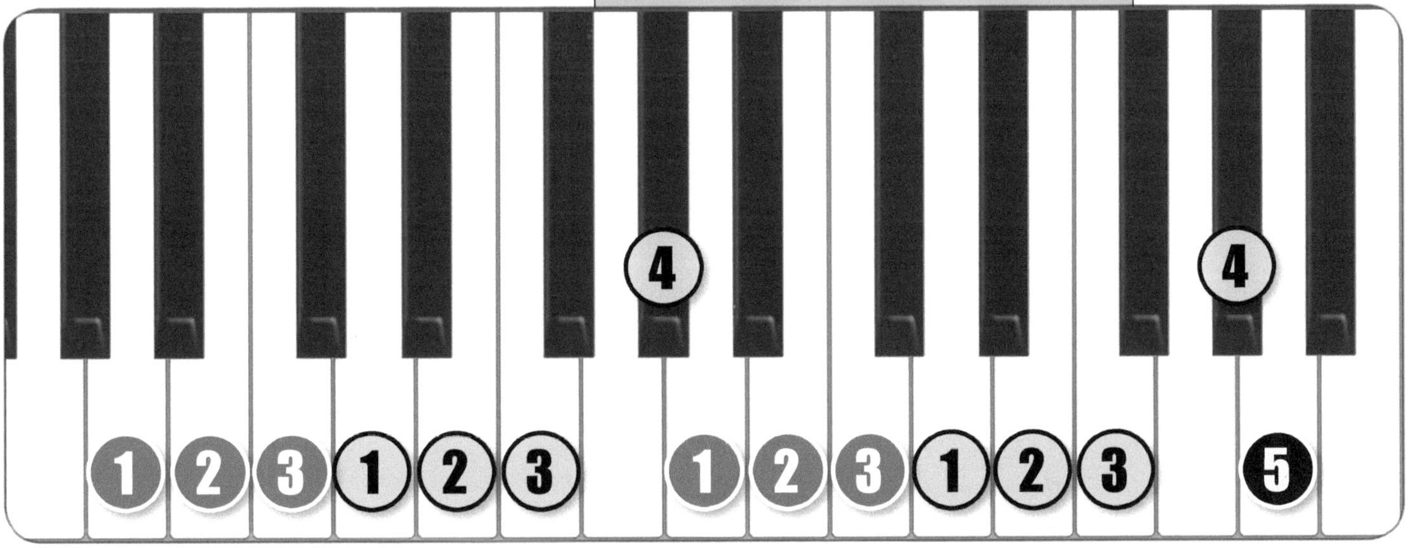

③ Twists

Brain hurtingly tough challenges

		1	2	3	4	5	6	7	8	9	10
Rhythm	**74**	☐	☐	☐	☐	☐	☐	☐	☐	☐	☐
Articulation	**76**	☐	☐	☐	☐	☐	☐	☐	☐	☐	☐
Dynamic	**78**	☐	☐	☐	☐	☐	☐	☐	☐	☐	☐
Ratio	**80**	☐	☐	☐	☐	☐	☐	☐	☐	–	–
Balance	**82**	☐	☐	☐	☐	☐	☐	☐	☐	–	–
Cacophony	**84**	☐	☐	☐	☐	☐	☐	☐	☐	☐	☐
Cascade	**86**	☐	☐	☐	☐	☐	☐	–	–	–	–
Interval	**88**	☐	☐	☐	☐	☐	☐	☐	☐	☐	☐
Contrary	**90**	☐	☐	☐	☐	☐	☐	–	–	–	–

Twists must be completed **2 hands together**

Track your Progress

Count your completed Challenges

- 1 ○ Dabbling
- 3 ○ Beginner
- **8 ○ Apprentice**
- 16 ○ Aspiring
- 27 ○ Experienced
- **41 ○ Skilled**
- 58 ○ Proficient
- 78 ○ Expert
- **101 ○ Master**
- 127 ○ Grandmaster
- 156 ○ Legendary
- **189 ○ Yours for life***

* You'll *never* forget this scale, even if you never practice it again.

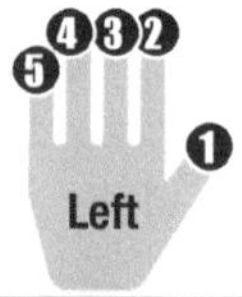

A Major

Very Easy | **Easy** | Moderate | Challenging | Difficult

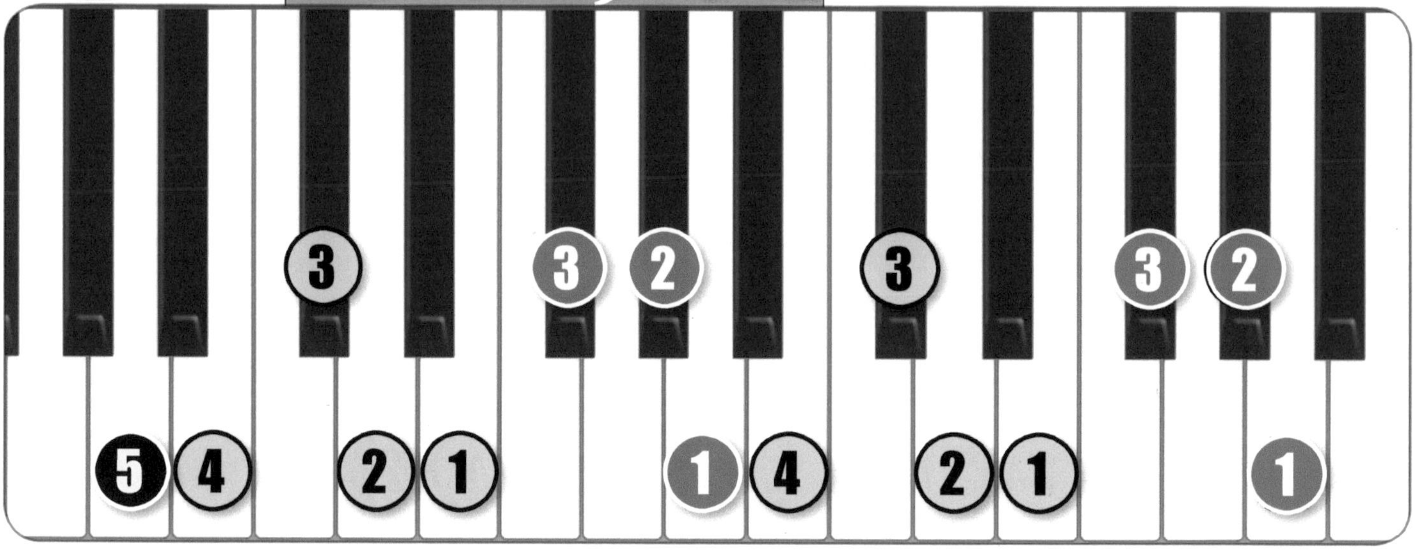

① Core Challenges

Start with these

Page		L	R	T
68	First Playthrough	☐	☐	☐
68	First from Memory	☐	☐	☐
68	First Contrary Motion	—	—	☐
68	4 Octave Tour	☐	☐	☐
69	Grand Tour	☐	☐	☐
69	Thrice is Nice	☐	☐	☐
69	10 in a Row	☐	☐	☐
69	3 Minute Quota	☐	☐	☐
70	3 Minute Tightrope	☐	☐	☐
70	Marathon Tightrope	☐	☐	☐
70	Witnessed by 6	☐	☐	☐
70	Lesson Startup	☐	☐	☐
71	Super Slow Motion	☐	☐	☐
71	Commentator	☐	☐	—
71	Splatmaster	☐	☐	—
72	By Feel Alone	☐	☐	☐
72	Tabletop Scale	☐	☐	☐
72	Repertoire	—	—	☐
72	Octave Collector	☐	☐	☐

L is Left Hand, **R** is Right Hand, **T** is Together

② Tempo Milestones

Gradually speeding it up

Metronome Setting	L	R	T	CM
♩=100 1 note per beat	☐	☐	☐	☐
♩=120 1 note per beat	☐	☐	☐	☐
♩=150 1 note per beat	☐	☐	☐	☐
♩=90 2 notes per beat	☐	☐	☐	☐
♩=105 2 notes per beat	☐	☐	☐	☐
♩=120 2 notes per beat	☐	☐	☐	☐
♩=135 2 notes per beat	☐	☐	☐	☐
♩=150 2 notes per beat	☐	☐	☐	☐
♩=80 4 notes per beat	☐	☐	☐	☐
♩=90 4 notes per beat	☐	☐	☐	☐
♩=100 4 notes per beat	☐	☐	☐	☐
♩=110 4 notes per beat	☐	☐	☐	☐
♩=120 4 notes per beat	☐	☐	☐	☐
♩=130 4 notes per beat	☐	☐	☐	☐
♩=140 4 notes per beat	☐	☐	☐	☐

CM is contrary motion. Contrary scales are 2 octaves, all others are 4 octaves. Must be **twice in a row correct**.

Very Easy | **Easy** | Moderate | Challenging | Difficult

A Major

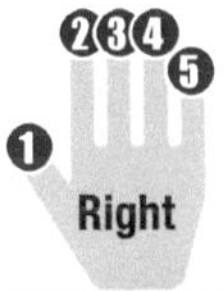

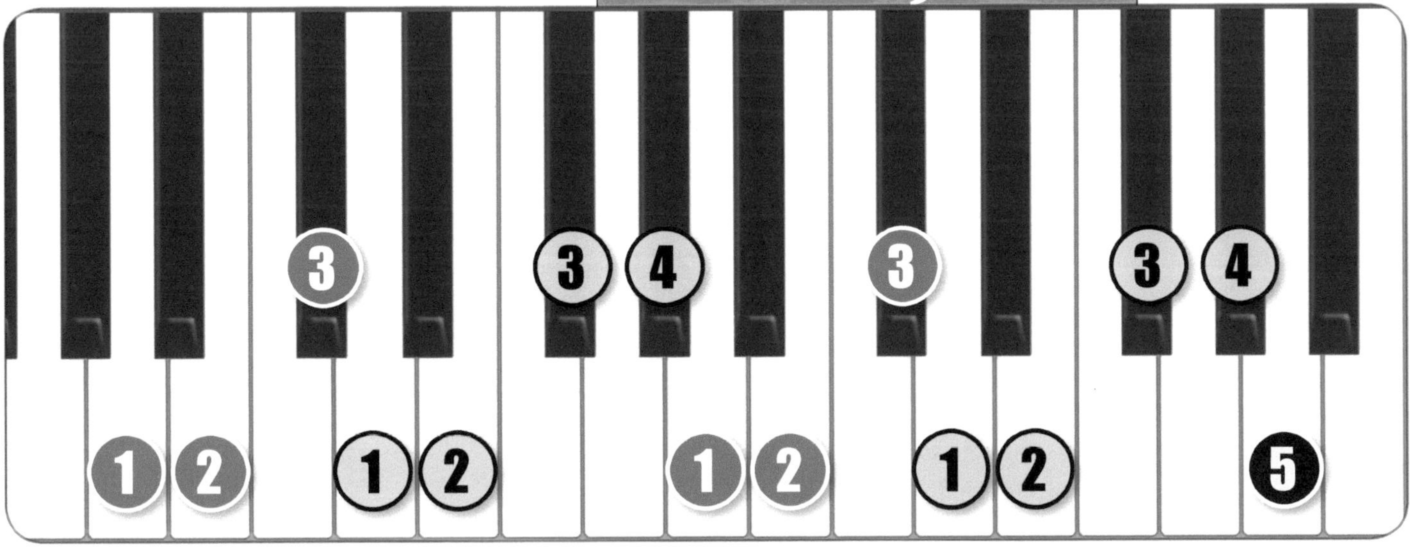

③ Twists

Brain hurtingly tough challenges

		1	2	3	4	5	6	7	8	9	10
Rhythm	**74**	☐	☐	☐	☐	☐	☐	☐	☐	☐	☐
Articulation	**76**	☐	☐	☐	☐	☐	☐	☐	☐	☐	☐
Dynamic	**78**	☐	☐	☐	☐	☐	☐	☐	☐	☐	☐
Ratio	**80**	☐	☐	☐	☐	☐	☐	☐	☐	–	–
Balance	**82**	☐	☐	☐	☐	☐	☐	☐	☐	–	–
Cacophony	**84**	☐	☐	☐	☐	☐	☐	☐	☐	☐	☐
Cascade	**86**	☐	☐	☐	☐	☐	☐	–	–	–	–
Interval	**88**	☐	☐	☐	☐	☐	☐	☐	☐	☐	☐
Contrary	**90**	☐	☐	☐	☐	☐	☐	–	–	–	–

Twists must be completed **2 hands together**

Track your Progress

Count your completed Challenges

- 1 ○ Dabbling
- 3 ○ Beginner
- **8 ○ Apprentice**
- 16 ○ Aspiring
- 27 ○ Experienced
- **41 ○ Skilled**
- 58 ○ Proficient
- 78 ○ Expert
- **101 ○ Master**
- 127 ○ Grandmaster
- 156 ○ Legendary
- **189 ○ Yours for life***

* You'll *never* forget this scale, even if you never practice it again.

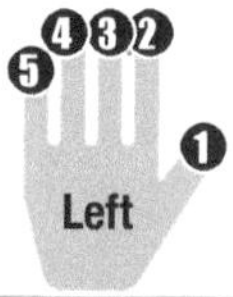

A#/Bb Minor

Very Easy | Easy | Moderate | Challenging | **Difficult**

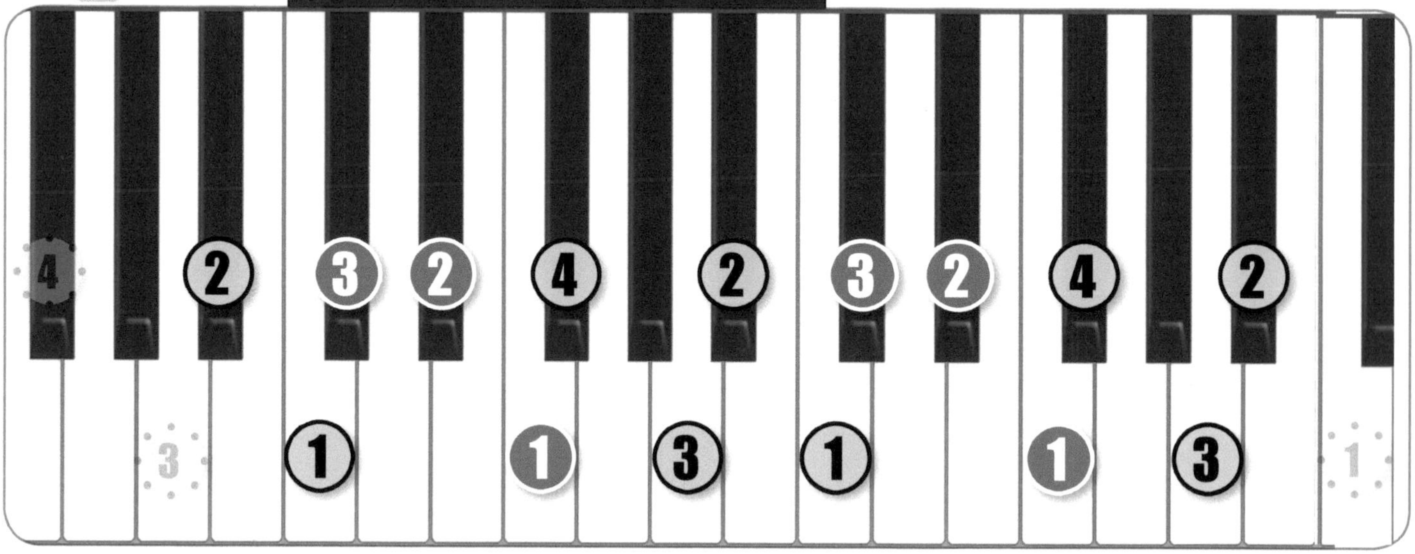

① Core Challenges

Start with these

Page		L	R	T
68	First Playthrough	☐	☐	☐
68	First from Memory	☐	☐	☐
68	First Contrary Motion	–	–	☐
68	4 Octave Tour	☐	☐	☐
69	Grand Tour	☐	☐	☐
69	Thrice is Nice	☐	☐	☐
69	10 in a Row	☐	☐	☐
69	3 Minute Quota	☐	☐	☐
70	3 Minute Tightrope	☐	☐	☐
70	Marathon Tightrope	☐	☐	☐
70	Witnessed by 6	☐	☐	☐
70	Lesson Startup	☐	☐	☐
71	Super Slow Motion	☐	☐	☐
71	Commentator	☐	☐	–
71	Splatmaster	☐	☐	–
72	By Feel Alone	☐	☐	☐
72	Tabletop Scale	☐	☐	☐
72	Repertoire	–	–	☐
72	Octave Collector	☐	☐	☐

L is Left Hand, **R** is Right Hand, **T** is Together

② Tempo Milestones

Gradually speeding it up

Metronome Setting	L	R	T	CM
♩=100 1 note per beat	☐	☐	☐	☐
♩=120 1 note per beat	☐	☐	☐	☐
♩=150 1 note per beat	☐	☐	☐	☐
♩=90 2 notes per beat	☐	☐	☐	☐
♩=105 2 notes per beat	☐	☐	☐	☐
♩=120 2 notes per beat	☐	☐	☐	☐
♩=135 2 notes per beat	☐	☐	☐	☐
♩=150 2 notes per beat	☐	☐	☐	☐
♩=80 4 notes per beat	☐	☐	☐	☐
♩=90 4 notes per beat	☐	☐	☐	☐
♩=100 4 notes per beat	☐	☐	☐	☐
♩=110 4 notes per beat	☐	☐	☐	☐
♩=120 4 notes per beat	☐	☐	☐	☐
♩=130 4 notes per beat	☐	☐	☐	☐
♩=140 4 notes per beat	☐	☐	☐	☐

CM is contrary motion. Contrary scales are 2 octaves, all others are 4 octaves. Must be **twice in a row correct**.

Very Easy | Easy | Moderate | Challenging | **Difficult**

A#/Bb Minor

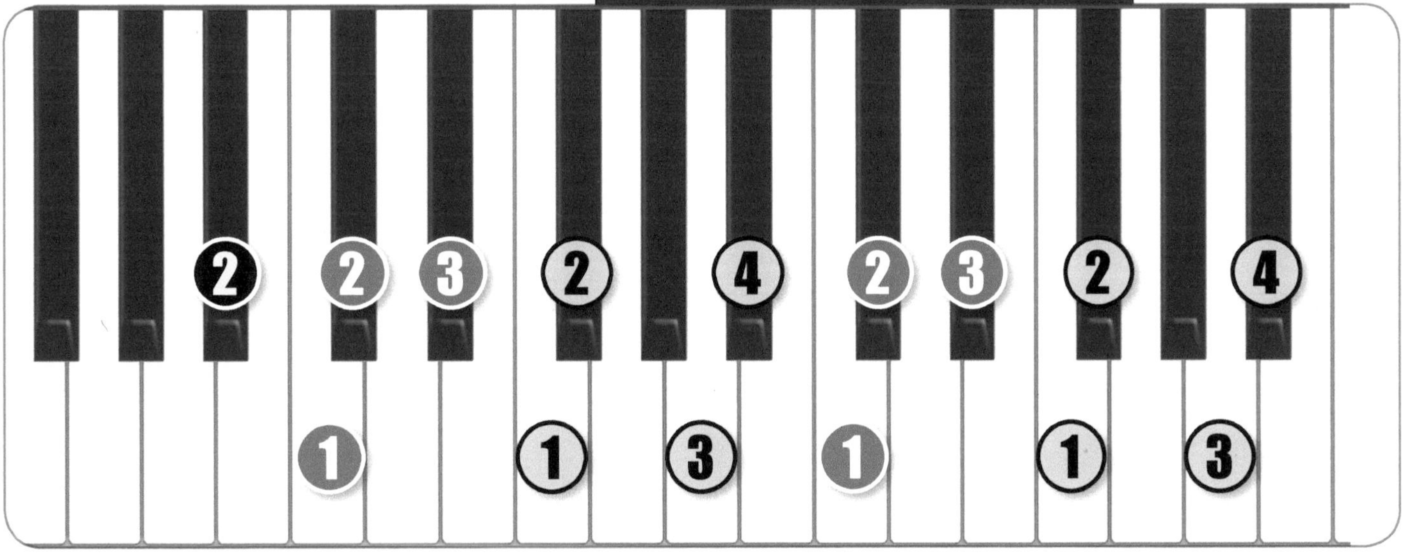

③ Twists

Brain hurtingly tough challenges

		1	2	3	4	5	6	7	8	9	10
Rhythm	**74**	☐	☐	☐	☐	☐	☐	☐	☐	☐	☐
Articulation	**76**	☐	☐	☐	☐	☐	☐	☐	☐	☐	☐
Dynamic	**78**	☐	☐	☐	☐	☐	☐	☐	☐	☐	☐
Ratio	**80**	☐	☐	☐	☐	☐	☐	☐	☐	–	–
Balance	**82**	☐	☐	☐	☐	☐	☐	☐	☐	–	–
Cacophony	**84**	☐	☐	☐	☐	☐	☐	☐	☐	☐	☐
Cascade	**86**	☐	☐	☐	☐	☐	☐	–	–	–	–
Interval	**88**	☐	☐	☐	☐	☐	☐	☐	☐	☐	☐
Contrary	**90**	☐	☐	☐	☐	☐	☐	–	–	–	–

Twists must be completed **2 hands together**

Track your Progress

Count your completed Challenges

- 1 ○ Dabbling
- 3 ○ Beginner
- **8 ○ Apprentice**
- 16 ○ Aspiring
- 27 ○ Experienced
- **41 ○ Skilled**
- 58 ○ Proficient
- 78 ○ Expert
- **101 ○ Master**
- 127 ○ Grandmaster
- 156 ○ Legendary
- **189 ○ Yours for life***

* You'll *never* forget this scale, even if you never practice it again.

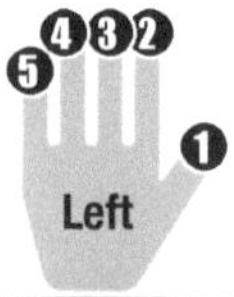

B♭ Major

Very Easy | Easy | **Moderate** | Challenging | Difficult

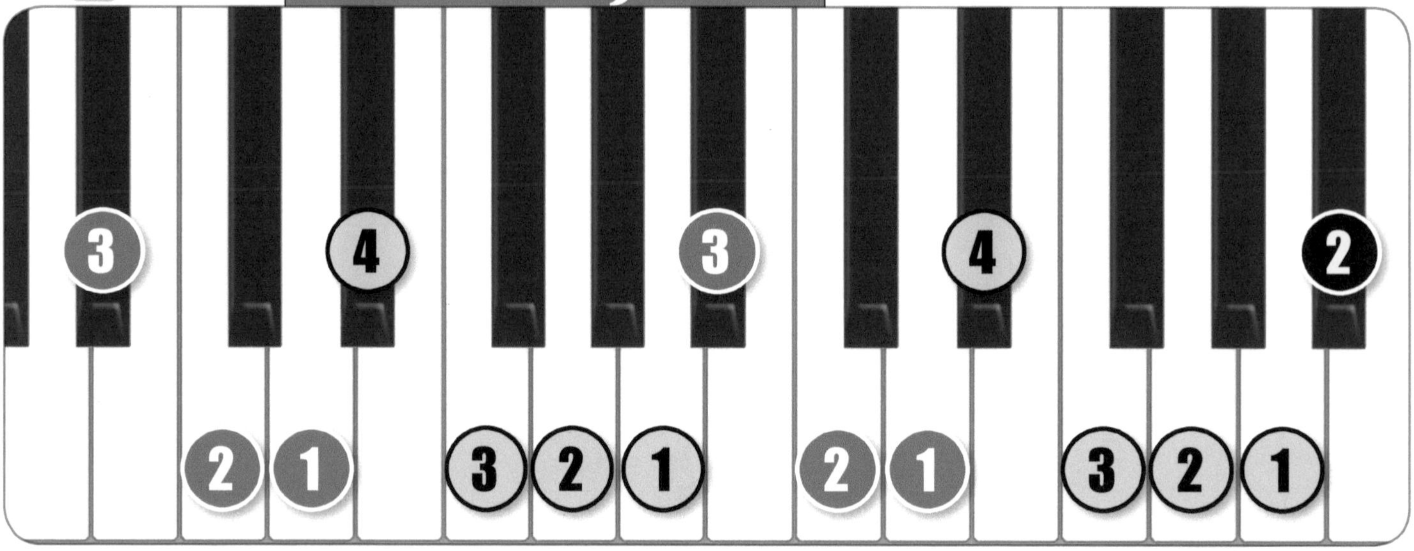

① Core Challenges

Start with these

Page		L	R	T
68	First Playthrough	☐	☐	☐
68	First from Memory	☐	☐	☐
68	First Contrary Motion	—	—	☐
68	4 Octave Tour	☐	☐	☐
69	Grand Tour	☐	☐	☐
69	Thrice is Nice	☐	☐	☐
69	10 in a Row	☐	☐	☐
69	3 Minute Quota	☐	☐	☐
70	3 Minute Tightrope	☐	☐	☐
70	Marathon Tightrope	☐	☐	☐
70	Witnessed by 6	☐	☐	☐
70	Lesson Startup	☐	☐	☐
71	Super Slow Motion	☐	☐	☐
71	Commentator	☐	☐	—
71	Splatmaster	☐	☐	—
72	By Feel Alone	☐	☐	☐
72	Tabletop Scale	☐	☐	☐
72	Repertoire	—	—	☐
72	Octave Collector	☐	☐	☐

L is Left Hand, **R** is Right Hand, **T** is Together

② Tempo Milestones

Gradually speeding it up

Metronome Setting	L	R	T	CM
♩=100 1 note per beat	☐	☐	☐	☐
♩=120 1 note per beat	☐	☐	☐	☐
♩=150 1 note per beat	☐	☐	☐	☐
♩=90 2 notes per beat	☐	☐	☐	☐
♩=105 2 notes per beat	☐	☐	☐	☐
♩=120 2 notes per beat	☐	☐	☐	☐
♩=135 2 notes per beat	☐	☐	☐	☐
♩=150 2 notes per beat	☐	☐	☐	☐
♩=80 4 notes per beat	☐	☐	☐	☐
♩=90 4 notes per beat	☐	☐	☐	☐
♩=100 4 notes per beat	☐	☐	☐	☐
♩=110 4 notes per beat	☐	☐	☐	☐
♩=120 4 notes per beat	☐	☐	☐	☐
♩=130 4 notes per beat	☐	☐	☐	☐
♩=140 4 notes per beat	☐	☐	☐	☐

CM is contrary motion. Contrary scales are 2 octaves, all others are 4 octaves. Must be **twice in a row correct**.

Very Easy | Easy | **Moderate** | Challenging | Difficult

B♭ Major

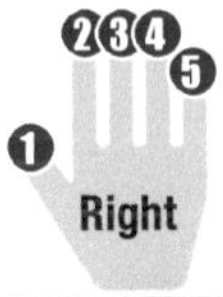

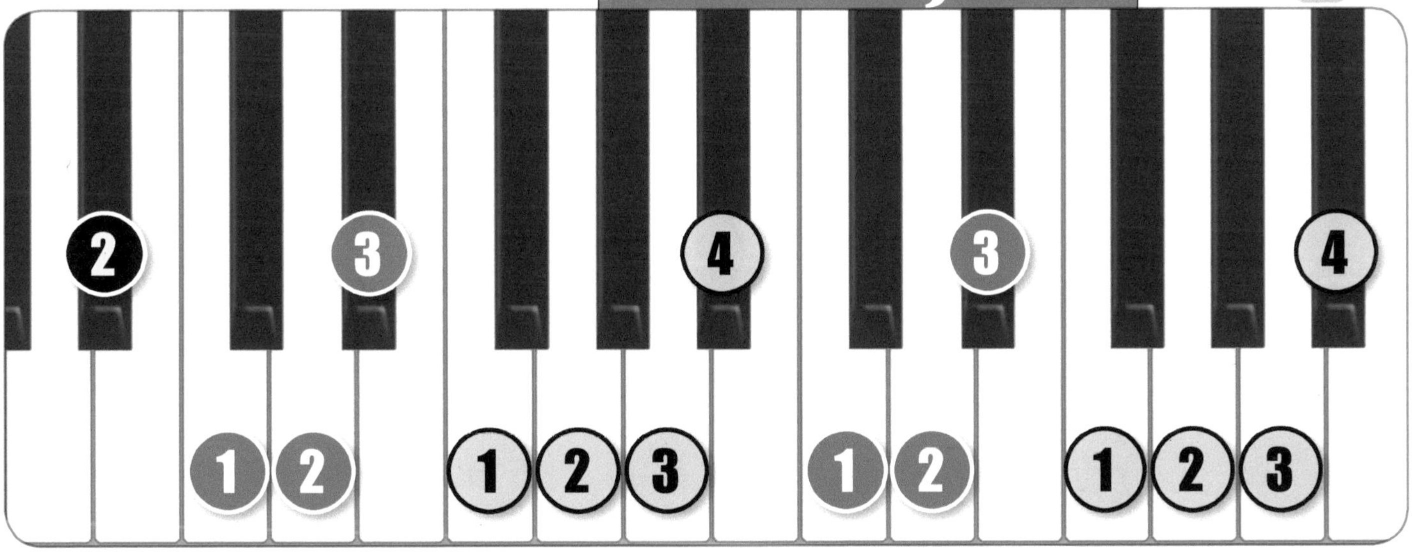

③ Twists

Brain hurtingly tough challenges

		1	2	3	4	5	6	7	8	9	10
Rhythm	**74**	☐	☐	☐	☐	☐	☐	☐	☐	☐	☐
Articulation	**76**	☐	☐	☐	☐	☐	☐	☐	☐	☐	☐
Dynamic	**78**	☐	☐	☐	☐	☐	☐	☐	☐	☐	☐
Ratio	**80**	☐	☐	☐	☐	☐	☐	☐	☐	–	–
Balance	**82**	☐	☐	☐	☐	☐	☐	☐	☐	–	–
Cacophony	**84**	☐	☐	☐	☐	☐	☐	☐	☐	☐	☐
Cascade	**86**	☐	☐	☐	☐	☐	☐	–	–	–	–
Interval	**88**	☐	☐	☐	☐	☐	☐	☐	☐	☐	☐
Contrary	**90**	☐	☐	☐	☐	☐	☐	–	–	–	–

Twists must be completed **2 hands together**

Track your Progress

Count your completed Challenges

- 1 ○ Dabbling
- 3 ○ Beginner
- **8 ○ Apprentice**
- 16 ○ Aspiring
- 27 ○ Experienced
- **41 ○ Skilled**
- 58 ○ Proficient
- 78 ○ Expert
- **101 ○ Master**
- 127 ○ Grandmaster
- 156 ○ Legendary
- **189 ○ Yours for life***

* You'll *never* forget this scale, even if you never practice it again.

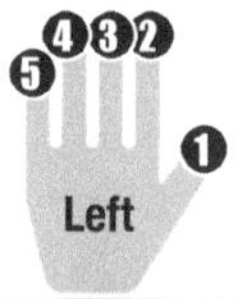

B Minor

Very Easy | Easy | Moderate | **Challenging** | Difficult

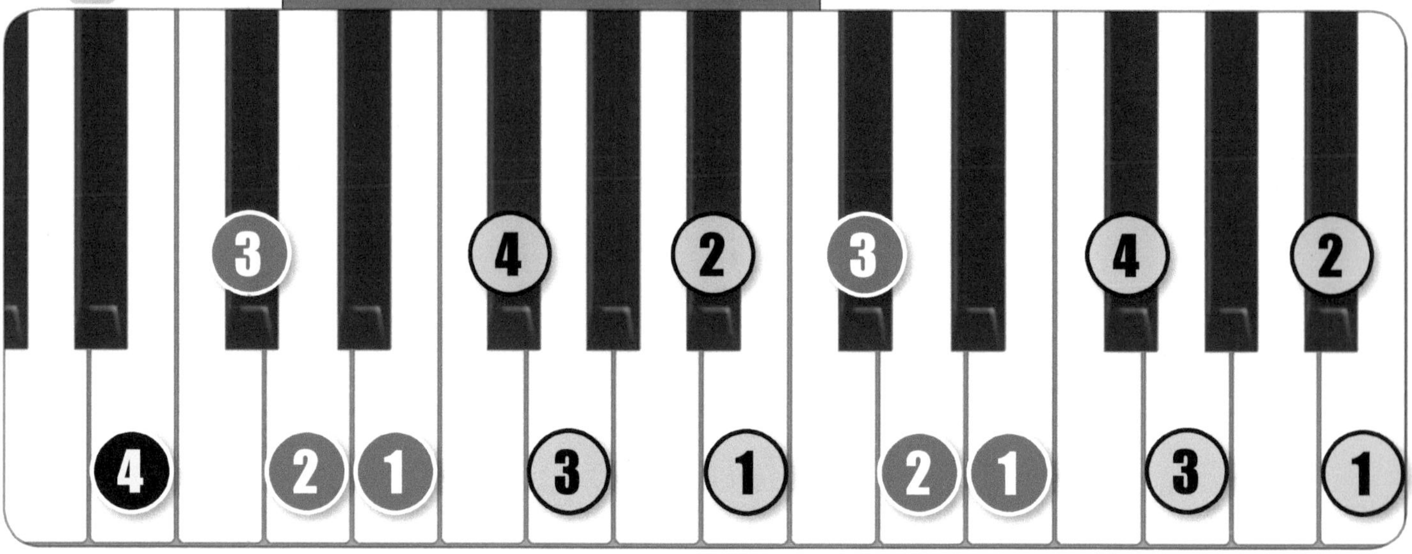

① Core Challenges

Start with these

Page		L	R	T
68	First Playthrough	☐	☐	☐
68	First from Memory	☐	☐	☐
68	First Contrary Motion	—	—	☐
68	4 Octave Tour	☐	☐	☐
69	Grand Tour	☐	☐	☐
69	Thrice is Nice	☐	☐	☐
69	10 in a Row	☐	☐	☐
69	3 Minute Quota	☐	☐	☐
70	3 Minute Tightrope	☐	☐	☐
70	Marathon Tightrope	☐	☐	☐
70	Witnessed by 6	☐	☐	☐
70	Lesson Startup	☐	☐	☐
71	Super Slow Motion	☐	☐	☐
71	Commentator	☐	☐	—
71	Splatmaster	☐	☐	—
72	By Feel Alone	☐	☐	☐
72	Tabletop Scale	☐	☐	☐
72	Repertoire	—	—	☐
72	Octave Collector	☐	☐	☐

L is Left Hand, **R** is Right Hand, **T** is Together

② Tempo Milestones

Gradually speeding it up

Metronome Setting	L	R	T	CM
♩=100 1 note per beat	☐	☐	☐	☐
♩=120 1 note per beat	☐	☐	☐	☐
♩=150 1 note per beat	☐	☐	☐	☐
♩=90 2 notes per beat	☐	☐	☐	☐
♩=105 2 notes per beat	☐	☐	☐	☐
♩=120 2 notes per beat	☐	☐	☐	☐
♩=135 2 notes per beat	☐	☐	☐	☐
♩=150 2 notes per beat	☐	☐	☐	☐
♩=80 4 notes per beat	☐	☐	☐	☐
♩=90 4 notes per beat	☐	☐	☐	☐
♩=100 4 notes per beat	☐	☐	☐	☐
♩=110 4 notes per beat	☐	☐	☐	☐
♩=120 4 notes per beat	☐	☐	☐	☐
♩=130 4 notes per beat	☐	☐	☐	☐
♩=140 4 notes per beat	☐	☐	☐	☐

CM is contrary motion. Contrary scales are 2 octaves, all others are 4 octaves. Must be **twice in a row correct**.

Very Easy | Easy | Moderate | **Challenging** | Difficult

B Minor

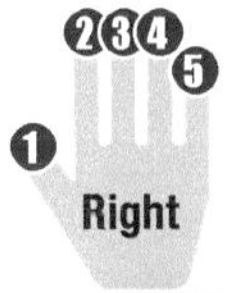

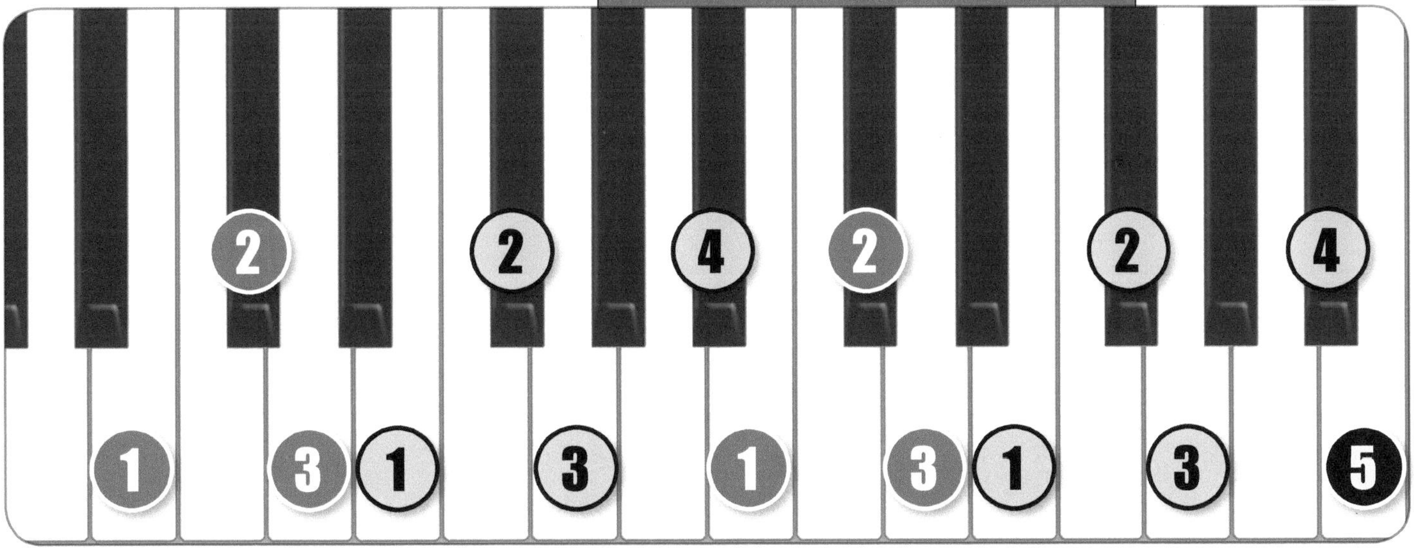

③ Twists

Brain hurtingly tough challenges

		1	2	3	4	5	6	7	8	9	10
Rhythm	**74**	☐	☐	☐	☐	☐	☐	☐	☐	☐	☐
Articulation	**76**	☐	☐	☐	☐	☐	☐	☐	☐	☐	☐
Dynamic	**78**	☐	☐	☐	☐	☐	☐	☐	☐	☐	☐
Ratio	**80**	☐	☐	☐	☐	☐	☐	☐	☐	–	–
Balance	**82**	☐	☐	☐	☐	☐	☐	☐	☐	–	–
Cacophony	**84**	☐	☐	☐	☐	☐	☐	☐	☐	☐	☐
Cascade	**86**	☐	☐	☐	☐	☐	☐	–	–	–	–
Interval	**88**	☐	☐	☐	☐	☐	☐	☐	☐	☐	☐
Contrary	**90**	☐	☐	☐	☐	☐	☐	–	–	–	–

Twists must be completed **2 hands together**

Track your Progress

Count your completed Challenges

- 1 ○ Dabbling
- 3 ○ Beginner
- **8 ○ Apprentice**
- 16 ○ Aspiring
- 27 ○ Experienced
- **41 ○ Skilled**
- 58 ○ Proficient
- 78 ○ Expert
- **101 ○ Master**
- 127 ○ Grandmaster
- 156 ○ Legendary
- **189 ○ Yours for life***

* You'll *never* forget this scale, even if you never practice it again.

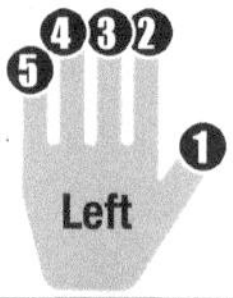

B/C^b Major

Very Easy | **Easy** | Moderate | Challenging | Difficult

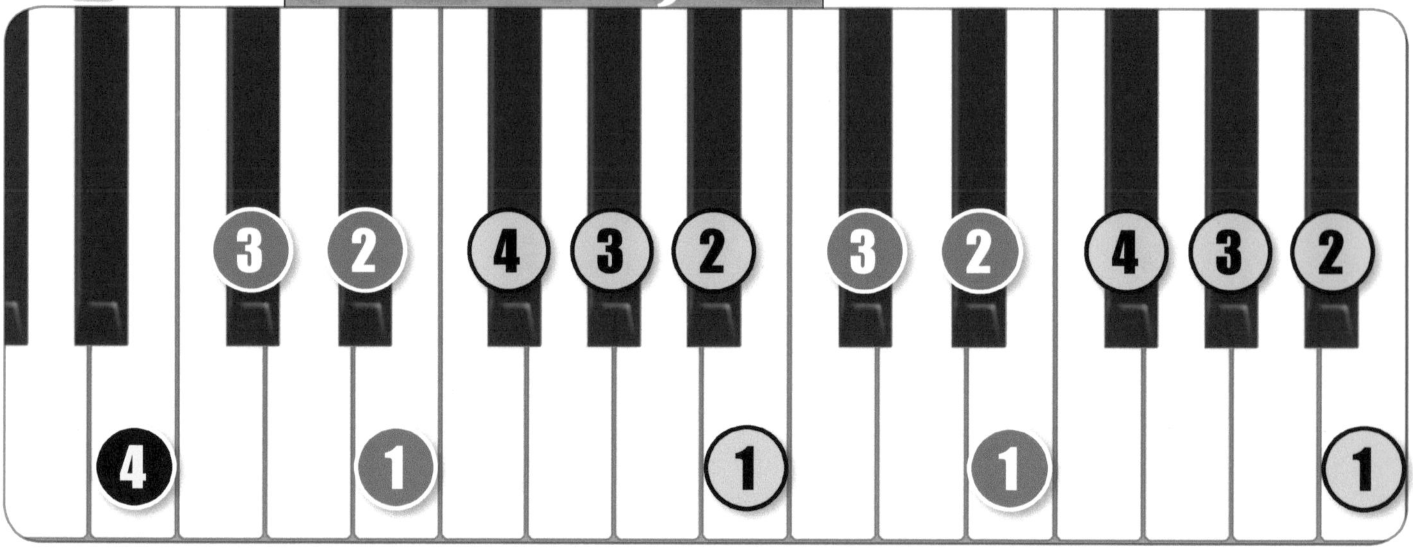

① Core Challenges

Start with these

Page		L	R	T
68	First Playthrough	☐	☐	☐
68	First from Memory	☐	☐	☐
68	First Contrary Motion	—	—	☐
68	4 Octave Tour	☐	☐	☐
69	Grand Tour	☐	☐	☐
69	Thrice is Nice	☐	☐	☐
69	10 in a Row	☐	☐	☐
69	3 Minute Quota	☐	☐	☐
70	3 Minute Tightrope	☐	☐	☐
70	Marathon Tightrope	☐	☐	☐
70	Witnessed by 6	☐	☐	☐
70	Lesson Startup	☐	☐	☐
71	Super Slow Motion	☐	☐	☐
71	Commentator	☐	☐	—
71	Splatmaster	☐	☐	—
72	By Feel Alone	☐	☐	☐
72	Tabletop Scale	☐	☐	☐
72	Repertoire	—	—	☐
72	Octave Collector	☐	☐	☐

L is Left Hand, **R** is Right Hand, **T** is Together

② Tempo Milestones

Gradually speeding it up

Metronome Setting	L	R	T	CM
♩=100 1 note per beat	☐	☐	☐	☐
♩=120 1 note per beat	☐	☐	☐	☐
♩=150 1 note per beat	☐	☐	☐	☐
♩=90 2 notes per beat	☐	☐	☐	☐
♩=105 2 notes per beat	☐	☐	☐	☐
♩=120 2 notes per beat	☐	☐	☐	☐
♩=135 2 notes per beat	☐	☐	☐	☐
♩=150 2 notes per beat	☐	☐	☐	☐
♩=80 4 notes per beat	☐	☐	☐	☐
♩=90 4 notes per beat	☐	☐	☐	☐
♩=100 4 notes per beat	☐	☐	☐	☐
♩=110 4 notes per beat	☐	☐	☐	☐
♩=120 4 notes per beat	☐	☐	☐	☐
♩=130 4 notes per beat	☐	☐	☐	☐
♩=140 4 notes per beat	☐	☐	☐	☐

CM is contrary motion. Contrary scales are 2 octaves, all others are 4 octaves. Must be **twice in a row correct**.

Very Easy | **Easy** | Moderate | Challenging | Difficult

B/C^{b} Major

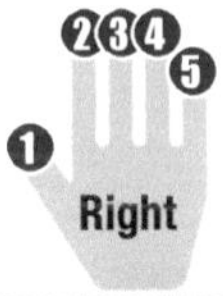

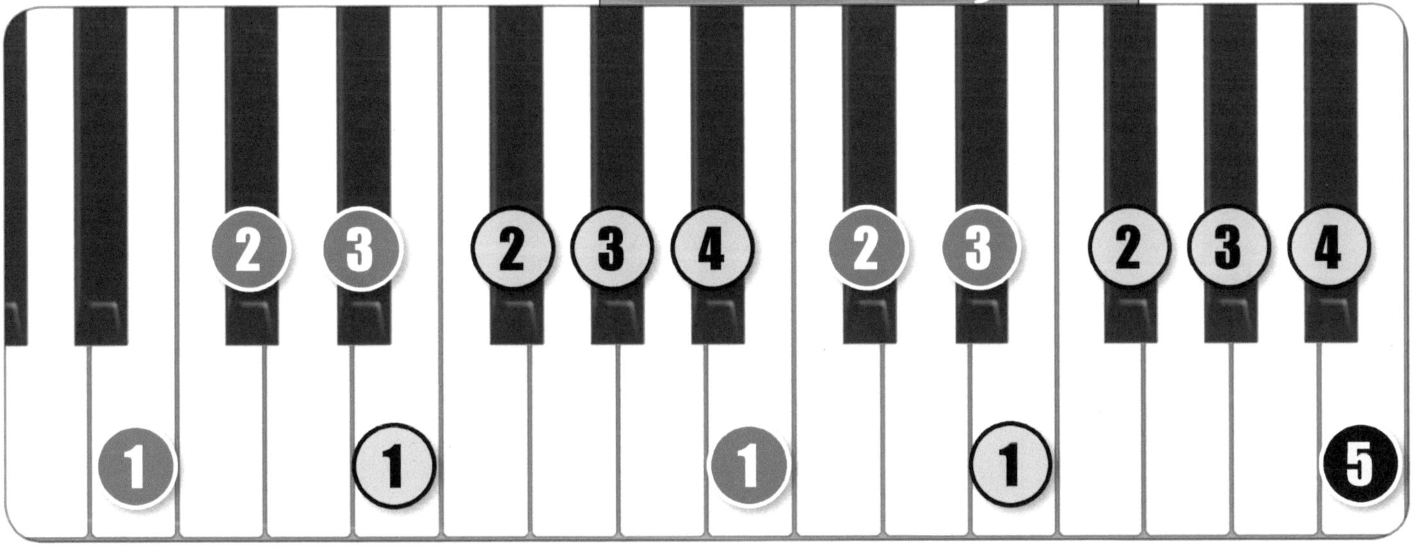

③ Twists

Brain hurtingly tough challenges

		1	2	3	4	5	6	7	8	9	10
Rhythm	**74**	☐	☐	☐	☐	☐	☐	☐	☐	☐	☐
Articulation	**76**	☐	☐	☐	☐	☐	☐	☐	☐	☐	☐
Dynamic	**78**	☐	☐	☐	☐	☐	☐	☐	☐	☐	☐
Ratio	**80**	☐	☐	☐	☐	☐	☐	☐	☐	–	–
Balance	**82**	☐	☐	☐	☐	☐	☐	☐	☐	–	–
Cacophony	**84**	☐	☐	☐	☐	☐	☐	☐	☐	☐	☐
Cascade	**86**	☐	☐	☐	☐	☐	☐	–	–	–	–
Interval	**88**	☐	☐	☐	☐	☐	☐	☐	☐	☐	☐
Contrary	**90**	☐	☐	☐	☐	☐	☐	–	–	–	–

Twists must be completed **2 hands together**

Track your Progress

Count your completed Challenges

1 ○ Dabbling
3 ○ Beginner
8 ○ Apprentice
16 ○ Aspiring
27 ○ Experienced
41 ○ Skilled
58 ○ Proficient
78 ○ Expert
101 ○ Master
127 ○ Grandmaster
156 ○ Legendary
189 ○ Yours for life*

* You'll *never* forget this scale, even if you never practice it again.

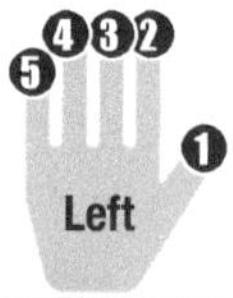

C Minor

Very Easy | **Easy** | Moderate | Challenging | Difficult

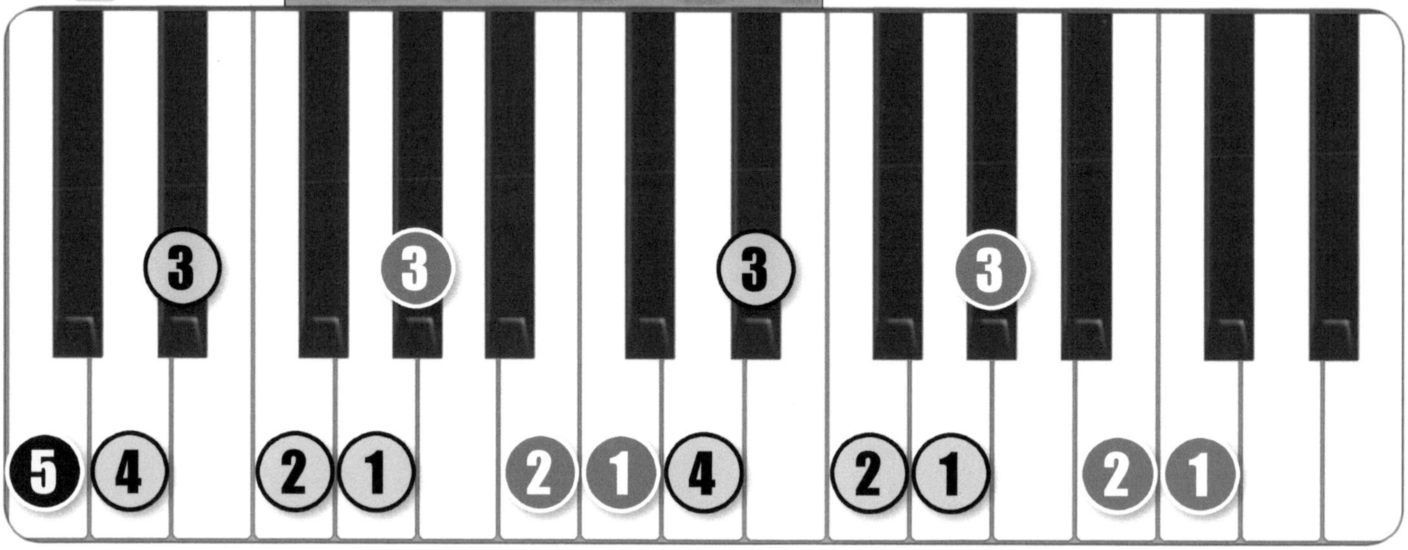

① Core Challenges

Start with these

Page		L	R	T
68	First Playthrough	☐	☐	☐
68	First from Memory	☐	☐	☐
68	First Contrary Motion	—	—	☐
68	4 Octave Tour	☐	☐	☐
69	Grand Tour	☐	☐	☐
69	Thrice is Nice	☐	☐	☐
69	10 in a Row	☐	☐	☐
69	3 Minute Quota	☐	☐	☐
70	3 Minute Tightrope	☐	☐	☐
70	Marathon Tightrope	☐	☐	☐
70	Witnessed by 6	☐	☐	☐
70	Lesson Startup	☐	☐	☐
71	Super Slow Motion	☐	☐	☐
71	Commentator	☐	☐	—
71	Splatmaster	☐	☐	—
72	By Feel Alone	☐	☐	☐
72	Tabletop Scale	☐	☐	☐
72	Repertoire	—	—	☐
72	Octave Collector	☐	☐	☐

L is Left Hand, **R** is Right Hand, **T** is Together

② Tempo Milestones

Gradually speeding it up

Metronome Setting	L	R	T	CM
♩=100 1 note per beat	☐	☐	☐	☐
♩=120 1 note per beat	☐	☐	☐	☐
♩=150 1 note per beat	☐	☐	☐	☐
♩=90 2 notes per beat	☐	☐	☐	☐
♩=105 2 notes per beat	☐	☐	☐	☐
♩=120 2 notes per beat	☐	☐	☐	☐
♩=135 2 notes per beat	☐	☐	☐	☐
♩=150 2 notes per beat	☐	☐	☐	☐
♩=80 4 notes per beat	☐	☐	☐	☐
♩=90 4 notes per beat	☐	☐	☐	☐
♩=100 4 notes per beat	☐	☐	☐	☐
♩=110 4 notes per beat	☐	☐	☐	☐
♩=120 4 notes per beat	☐	☐	☐	☐
♩=130 4 notes per beat	☐	☐	☐	☐
♩=140 4 notes per beat	☐	☐	☐	☐

CM is contrary motion. Contrary scales are 2 octaves, all others are 4 octaves. Must be **twice in a row correct**.

Very Easy | **Easy** | Moderate | Challenging | Difficult

C Minor

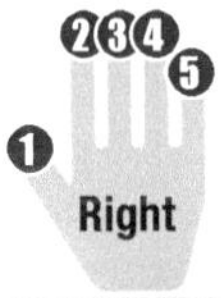

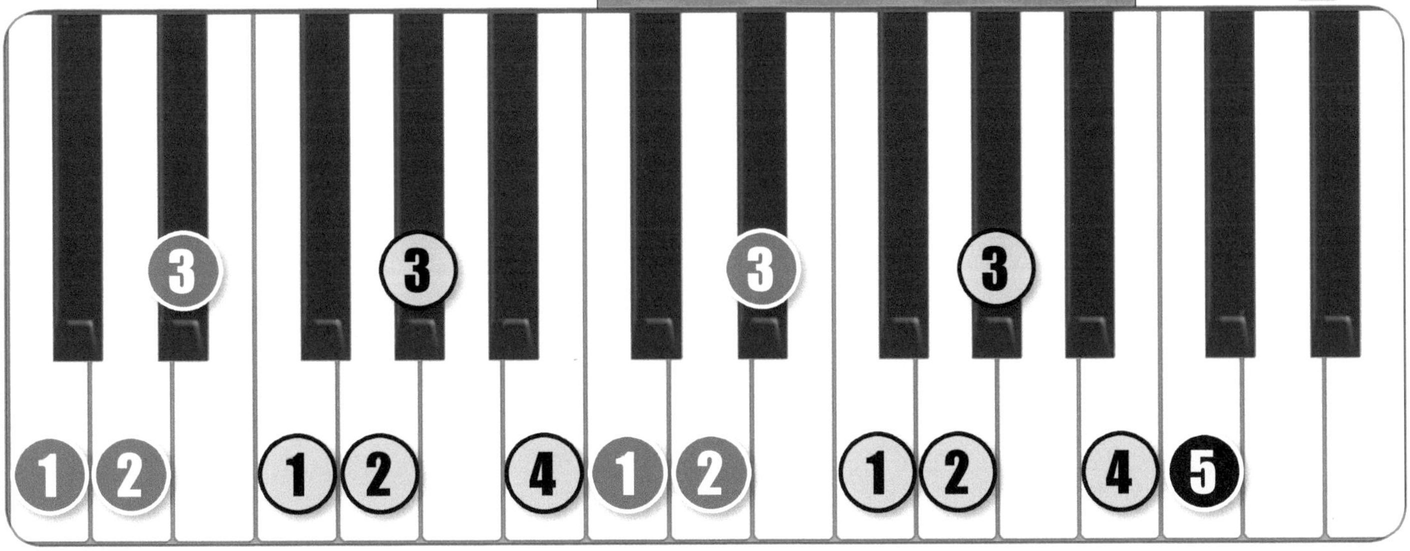

③ Twists

Brain hurtingly tough challenges

		1	2	3	4	5	6	7	8	9	10
Rhythm	**74**	☐	☐	☐	☐	☐	☐	☐	☐	☐	☐
Articulation	**76**	☐	☐	☐	☐	☐	☐	☐	☐	☐	☐
Dynamic	**78**	☐	☐	☐	☐	☐	☐	☐	☐	☐	☐
Ratio	**80**	☐	☐	☐	☐	☐	☐	☐	☐	–	–
Balance	**82**	☐	☐	☐	☐	☐	☐	☐	☐	–	–
Cacophony	**84**	☐	☐	☐	☐	☐	☐	☐	☐	☐	☐
Cascade	**86**	☐	☐	☐	☐	☐	☐	–	–	–	–
Interval	**88**	☐	☐	☐	☐	☐	☐	☐	☐	☐	☐
Contrary	**90**	☐	☐	☐	☐	☐	☐	–	–	–	–

Twists must be completed **2 hands together**

Track your Progress

Count your completed Challenges

- 1 ○ Dabbling
- 3 ○ Beginner
- **8 ○ Apprentice**
- 16 ○ Aspiring
- 27 ○ Experienced
- **41 ○ Skilled**
- 58 ○ Proficient
- 78 ○ Expert
- **101 ○ Master**
- 127 ○ Grandmaster
- 156 ○ Legendary
- **189 ○ Yours for life***

* You'll *never* forget this scale, even if you never practice it again.

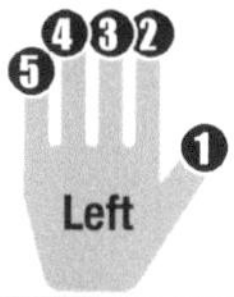

C Major

Very Easy | Easy | Moderate | Challenging | Difficult

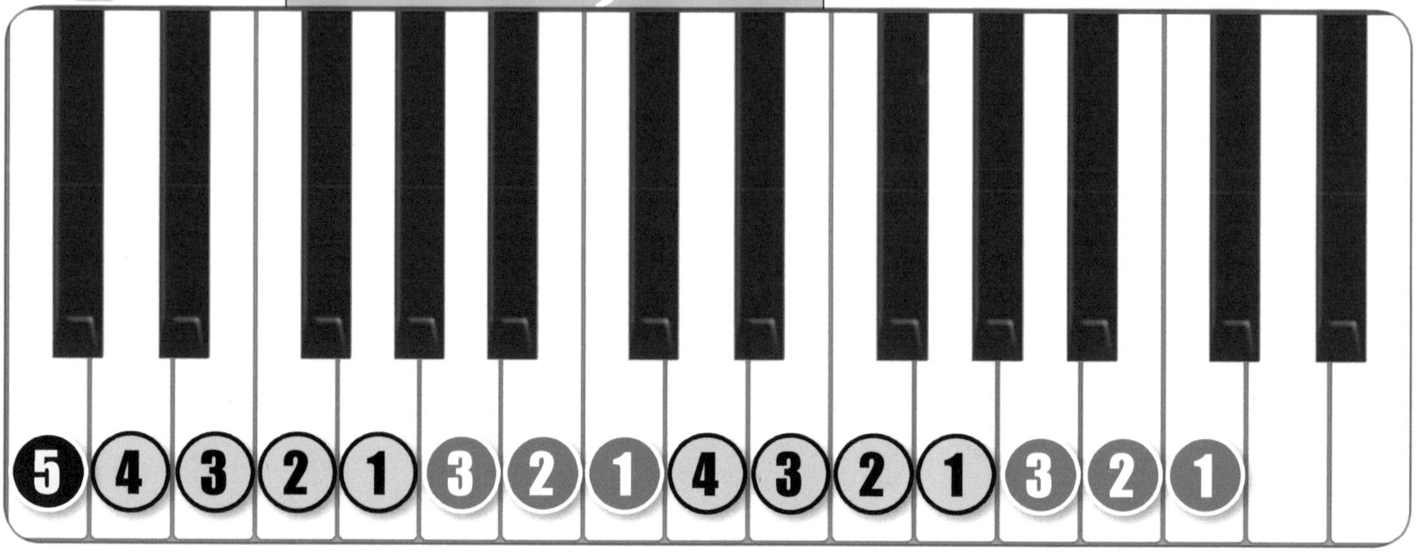

① Core Challenges

Start with these

Page		L	R	T
68	First Playthrough	☐	☐	☐
68	First from Memory	☐	☐	☐
68	First Contrary Motion	—	—	☐
68	4 Octave Tour	☐	☐	☐
69	Grand Tour	☐	☐	☐
69	Thrice is Nice	☐	☐	☐
69	10 in a Row	☐	☐	☐
69	3 Minute Quota	☐	☐	☐
70	3 Minute Tightrope	☐	☐	☐
70	Marathon Tightrope	☐	☐	☐
70	Witnessed by 6	☐	☐	☐
70	Lesson Startup	☐	☐	☐
71	Super Slow Motion	☐	☐	☐
71	Commentator	☐	☐	—
71	Splatmaster	☐	☐	—
72	By Feel Alone	☐	☐	☐
72	Tabletop Scale	☐	☐	☐
72	Repertoire	—	—	☐
72	Octave Collector	☐	☐	☐

L is Left Hand, **R** is Right Hand, **T** is Together

② Tempo Milestones

Gradually speeding it up

Metronome Setting	L	R	T	CM
♩=100 1 note per beat	☐	☐	☐	☐
♩=120 1 note per beat	☐	☐	☐	☐
♩=150 1 note per beat	☐	☐	☐	☐
♩=90 2 notes per beat	☐	☐	☐	☐
♩=105 2 notes per beat	☐	☐	☐	☐
♩=120 2 notes per beat	☐	☐	☐	☐
♩=135 2 notes per beat	☐	☐	☐	☐
♩=150 2 notes per beat	☐	☐	☐	☐
♩=80 4 notes per beat	☐	☐	☐	☐
♩=90 4 notes per beat	☐	☐	☐	☐
♩=100 4 notes per beat	☐	☐	☐	☐
♩=110 4 notes per beat	☐	☐	☐	☐
♩=120 4 notes per beat	☐	☐	☐	☐
♩=130 4 notes per beat	☐	☐	☐	☐
♩=140 4 notes per beat	☐	☐	☐	☐

CM is contrary motion. Contrary scales are 2 octaves, all others are 4 octaves. Must be **twice in a row correct**.

Very Easy | Easy | Moderate | Challenging | Difficult

C Major

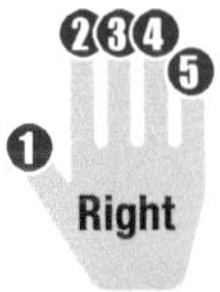

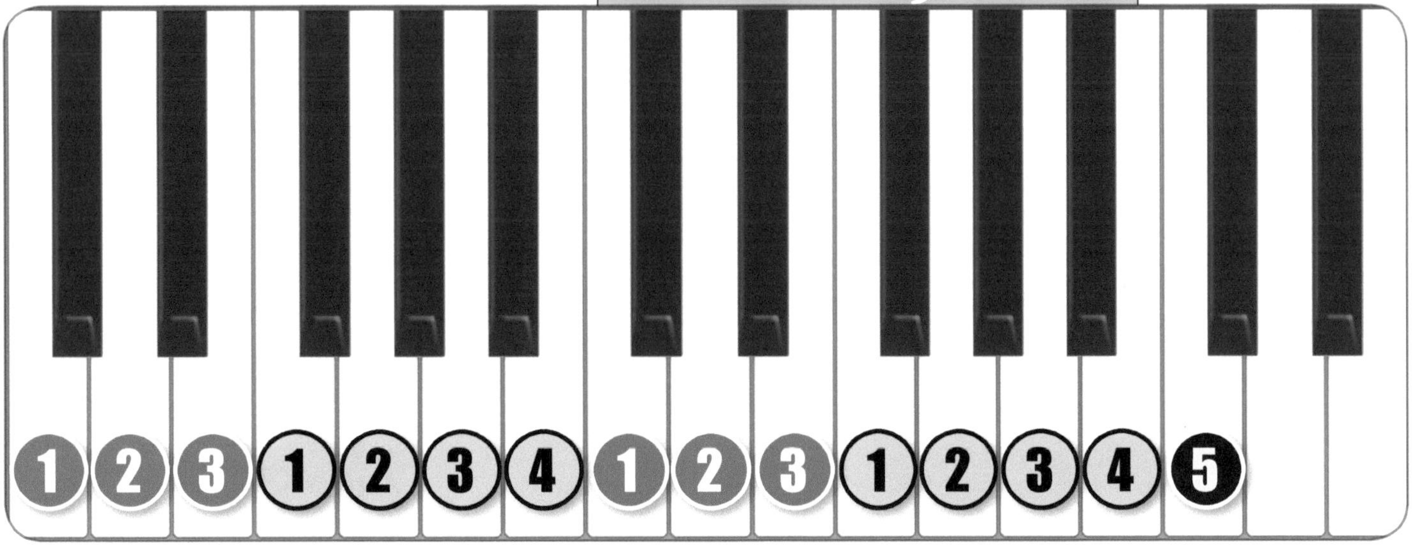

③ Twists

Brain hurtingly tough challenges

		1	2	3	4	5	6	7	8	9	10
Rhythm	**74**	☐	☐	☐	☐	☐	☐	☐	☐	☐	☐
Articulation	**76**	☐	☐	☐	☐	☐	☐	☐	☐	☐	☐
Dynamic	**78**	☐	☐	☐	☐	☐	☐	☐	☐	☐	☐
Ratio	**80**	☐	☐	☐	☐	☐	☐	☐	☐	–	–
Balance	**82**	☐	☐	☐	☐	☐	☐	☐	☐	–	–
Cacophony	**84**	☐	☐	☐	☐	☐	☐	☐	☐	☐	☐
Cascade	**86**	☐	☐	☐	☐	☐	☐	–	–	–	–
Interval	**88**	☐	☐	☐	☐	☐	☐	☐	☐	☐	☐
Contrary	**90**	☐	☐	☐	☐	☐	☐	–	–	–	–

Twists must be completed **2 hands together**

Track your Progress

Count your completed Challenges

- 1 ○ Dabbling
- 3 ○ Beginner
- **8 ○ Apprentice**
- 16 ○ Aspiring
- 27 ○ Experienced
- **41 ○ Skilled**
- 58 ○ Proficient
- 78 ○ Expert
- **101 ○ Master**
- 127 ○ Grandmaster
- 156 ○ Legendary
- **189 ○ Yours for life***

* You'll ***never*** forget this scale, even if you never practice it again.

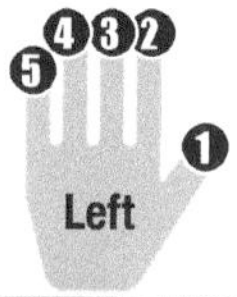

C# Minor

Very Easy | Easy | Moderate | Challenging | **Difficult**

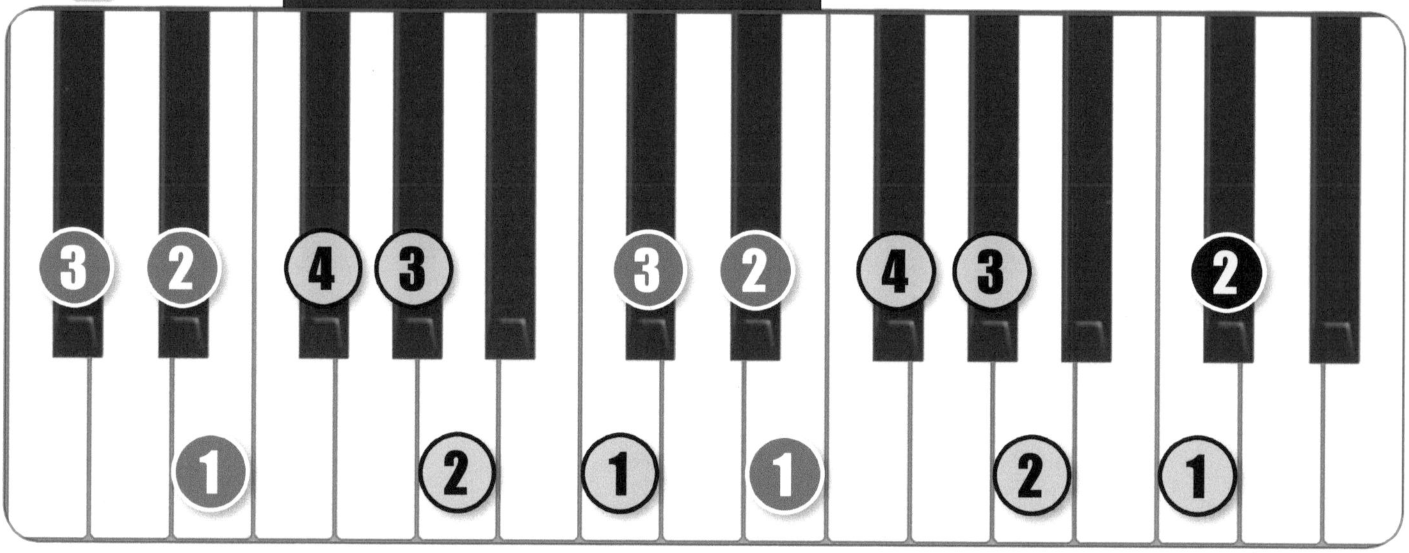

① Core Challenges

Start with these

Page		L	R	T
68	First Playthrough	☐	☐	☐
68	First from Memory	☐	☐	☐
68	First Contrary Motion	—	—	☐
68	4 Octave Tour	☐	☐	☐
69	Grand Tour	☐	☐	☐
69	Thrice is Nice	☐	☐	☐
69	10 in a Row	☐	☐	☐
69	3 Minute Quota	☐	☐	☐
70	3 Minute Tightrope	☐	☐	☐
70	Marathon Tightrope	☐	☐	☐
70	Witnessed by 6	☐	☐	☐
70	Lesson Startup	☐	☐	☐
71	Super Slow Motion	☐	☐	☐
71	Commentator	☐	☐	—
71	Splatmaster	☐	☐	—
72	By Feel Alone	☐	☐	☐
72	Tabletop Scale	☐	☐	☐
72	Repertoire	—	—	☐
72	Octave Collector	☐	☐	☐

L is Left Hand, **R** is Right Hand, **T** is Together

② Tempo Milestones

Gradually speeding it up

Metronome Setting	L	R	T	CM
♩=100 1 note per beat	☐	☐	☐	☐
♩=120 1 note per beat	☐	☐	☐	☐
♩=150 1 note per beat	☐	☐	☐	☐
♩=90 2 notes per beat	☐	☐	☐	☐
♩=105 2 notes per beat	☐	☐	☐	☐
♩=120 2 notes per beat	☐	☐	☐	☐
♩=135 2 notes per beat	☐	☐	☐	☐
♩=150 2 notes per beat	☐	☐	☐	☐
♩=80 4 notes per beat	☐	☐	☐	☐
♩=90 4 notes per beat	☐	☐	☐	☐
♩=100 4 notes per beat	☐	☐	☐	☐
♩=110 4 notes per beat	☐	☐	☐	☐
♩=120 4 notes per beat	☐	☐	☐	☐
♩=130 4 notes per beat	☐	☐	☐	☐
♩=140 4 notes per beat	☐	☐	☐	☐

CM is contrary motion. Contrary scales are 2 octaves, all others are 4 octaves. Must be **twice in a row correct**.

Very Easy | Easy | Moderate | Challenging | **Difficult**

C# Minor

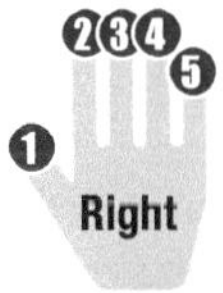

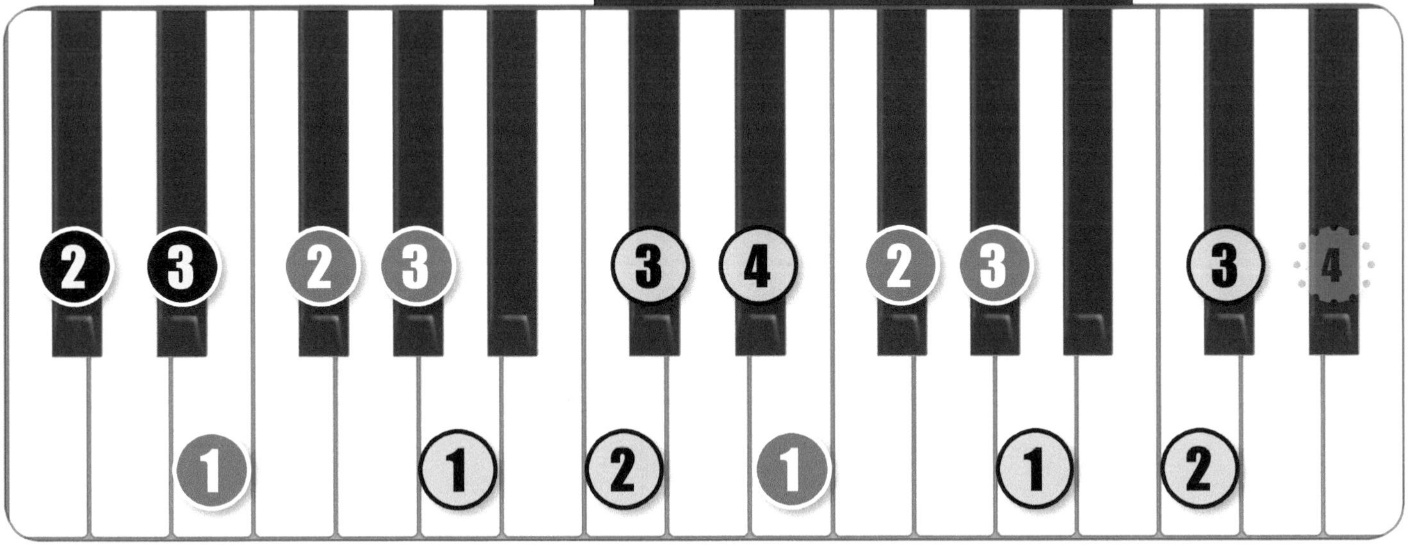

③ Twists

Brain hurtingly tough challenges

		1	2	3	4	5	6	7	8	9	10
Rhythm	**74**	☐	☐	☐	☐	☐	☐	☐	☐	☐	☐
Articulation	**76**	☐	☐	☐	☐	☐	☐	☐	☐	☐	☐
Dynamic	**78**	☐	☐	☐	☐	☐	☐	☐	☐	☐	☐
Ratio	**80**	☐	☐	☐	☐	☐	☐	☐	☐	–	–
Balance	**82**	☐	☐	☐	☐	☐	☐	☐	☐	–	–
Cacophony	**84**	☐	☐	☐	☐	☐	☐	☐	☐	☐	☐
Cascade	**86**	☐	☐	☐	☐	☐	☐	–	–	–	–
Interval	**88**	☐	☐	☐	☐	☐	☐	☐	☐	☐	☐
Contrary	**90**	☐	☐	☐	☐	☐	☐	–	–	–	–

Twists must be completed **2 hands together**

Track your Progress

Count your completed Challenges

- 1 ○ Dabbling
- 3 ○ Beginner
- **8 ○ Apprentice**
- 16 ○ Aspiring
- 27 ○ Experienced
- **41 ○ Skilled**
- 58 ○ Proficient
- 78 ○ Expert
- **101 ○ Master**
- 127 ○ Grandmaster
- 156 ○ Legendary
- **189 ○ Yours for life***

* You'll *never* forget this scale, even if you never practice it again.

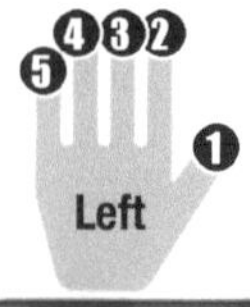

$C^{\#}/D^{b}$ Major

Very Easy | Easy | Moderate | **Challenging** | Difficult

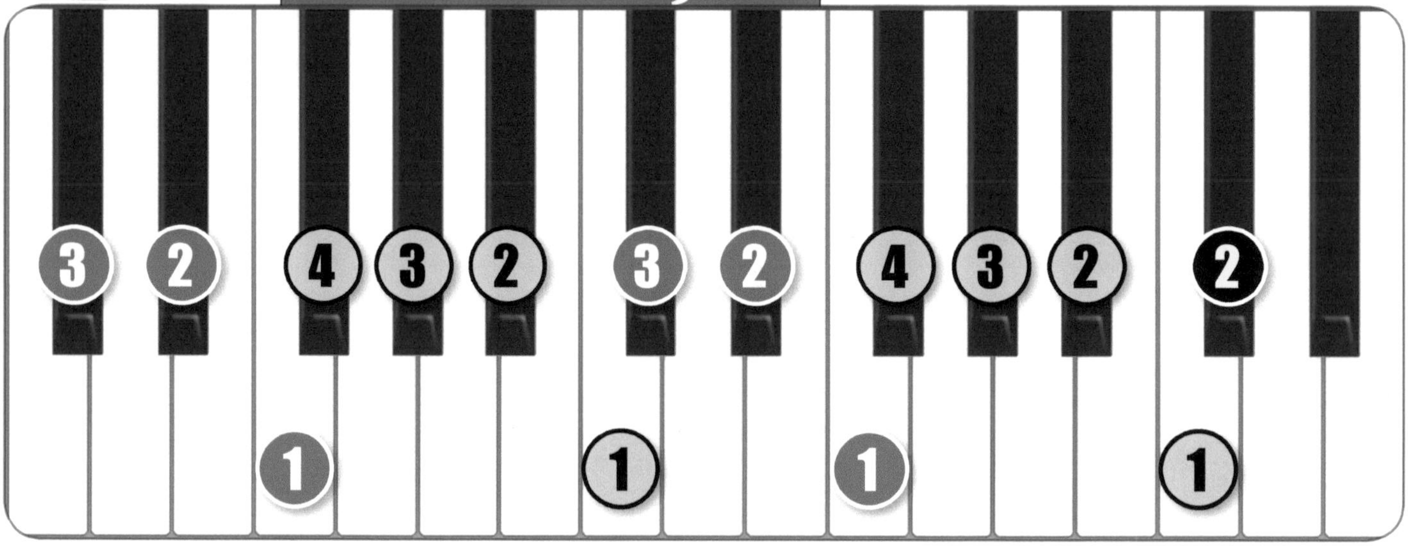

① Core Challenges

Start with these

Page		L	R	T
68	First Playthrough	☐	☐	☐
68	First from Memory	☐	☐	☐
68	First Contrary Motion	—	—	☐
68	4 Octave Tour	☐	☐	☐
69	Grand Tour	☐	☐	☐
69	Thrice is Nice	☐	☐	☐
69	10 in a Row	☐	☐	☐
69	3 Minute Quota	☐	☐	☐
70	3 Minute Tightrope	☐	☐	☐
70	Marathon Tightrope	☐	☐	☐
70	Witnessed by 6	☐	☐	☐
70	Lesson Startup	☐	☐	☐
71	Super Slow Motion	☐	☐	☐
71	Commentator	☐	☐	—
71	Splatmaster	☐	☐	—
72	By Feel Alone	☐	☐	☐
72	Tabletop Scale	☐	☐	☐
72	Repertoire	—	—	☐
72	Octave Collector	☐	☐	☐

L is Left Hand, **R** is Right Hand, **T** is Together

② Tempo Milestones

Gradually speeding it up

Metronome Setting	L	R	T	CM
♩=100 1 note per beat	☐	☐	☐	☐
♩=120 1 note per beat	☐	☐	☐	☐
♩=150 1 note per beat	☐	☐	☐	☐
♩=90 2 notes per beat	☐	☐	☐	☐
♩=105 2 notes per beat	☐	☐	☐	☐
♩=120 2 notes per beat	☐	☐	☐	☐
♩=135 2 notes per beat	☐	☐	☐	☐
♩=150 2 notes per beat	☐	☐	☐	☐
♩=80 4 notes per beat	☐	☐	☐	☐
♩=90 4 notes per beat	☐	☐	☐	☐
♩=100 4 notes per beat	☐	☐	☐	☐
♩=110 4 notes per beat	☐	☐	☐	☐
♩=120 4 notes per beat	☐	☐	☐	☐
♩=130 4 notes per beat	☐	☐	☐	☐
♩=140 4 notes per beat	☐	☐	☐	☐

CM is contrary motion. Contrary scales are 2 octaves, all others are 4 octaves. Must be **twice in a row correct**.

Very Easy | Easy | Moderate | **Challenging** | Difficult

C#/Db Major

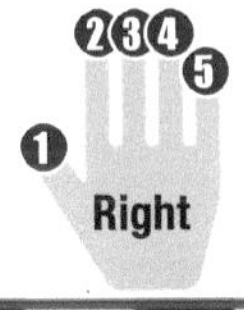

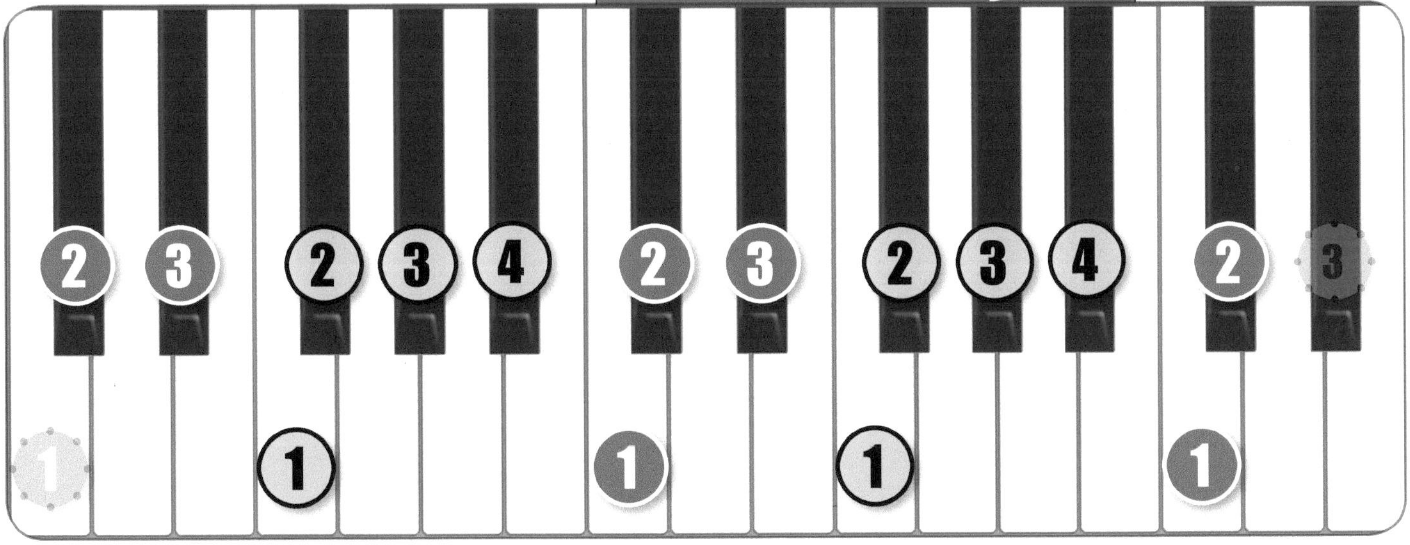

③ Twists

Brain hurtingly tough challenges

		1	2	3	4	5	6	7	8	9	10
Rhythm	**74**	☐	☐	☐	☐	☐	☐	☐	☐	☐	☐
Articulation	**76**	☐	☐	☐	☐	☐	☐	☐	☐	☐	☐
Dynamic	**78**	☐	☐	☐	☐	☐	☐	☐	☐	☐	☐
Ratio	**80**	☐	☐	☐	☐	☐	☐	☐	☐	–	–
Balance	**82**	☐	☐	☐	☐	☐	☐	☐	☐	–	–
Cacophony	**84**	☐	☐	☐	☐	☐	☐	☐	☐	☐	☐
Cascade	**86**	☐	☐	☐	☐	☐	☐	–	–	–	–
Interval	**88**	☐	☐	☐	☐	☐	☐	☐	☐	☐	☐
Contrary	**90**	☐	☐	☐	☐	☐	☐	–	–	–	–

Twists must be completed **2 hands together**

Track your Progress

Count your completed Challenges

- 1 ○ Dabbling
- 3 ○ Beginner
- **8 ○ Apprentice**
- 16 ○ Aspiring
- 27 ○ Experienced
- **41 ○ Skilled**
- 58 ○ Proficient
- 78 ○ Expert
- **101 ○ Master**
- 127 ○ Grandmaster
- 156 ○ Legendary
- **189 ○ Yours for life***

* You'll *never* forget this scale, even if you never practice it again.

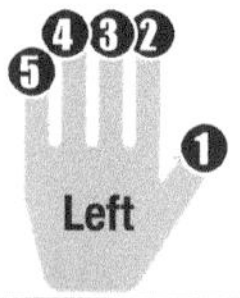

D Minor

Very Easy | **Easy** | Moderate | Challenging | Difficult

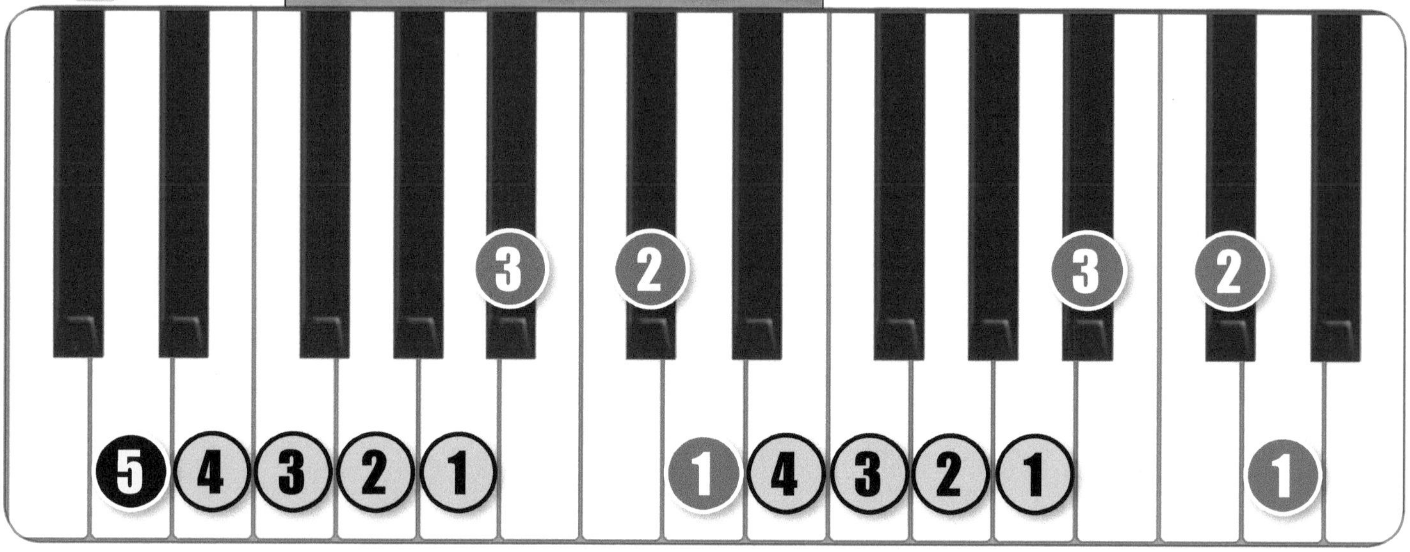

① Core Challenges

Start with these

Page		L	R	T
68	First Playthrough	☐	☐	☐
68	First from Memory	☐	☐	☐
68	First Contrary Motion	–	–	☐
68	4 Octave Tour	☐	☐	☐
69	Grand Tour	☐	☐	☐
69	Thrice is Nice	☐	☐	☐
69	10 in a Row	☐	☐	☐
69	3 Minute Quota	☐	☐	☐
70	3 Minute Tightrope	☐	☐	☐
70	Marathon Tightrope	☐	☐	☐
70	Witnessed by 6	☐	☐	☐
70	Lesson Startup	☐	☐	☐
71	Super Slow Motion	☐	☐	☐
71	Commentator	☐	☐	–
71	Splatmaster	☐	☐	–
72	By Feel Alone	☐	☐	☐
72	Tabletop Scale	☐	☐	☐
72	Repertoire	–	–	☐
72	Octave Collector	☐	☐	☐

L is Left Hand, **R** is Right Hand, **T** is Together

② Tempo Milestones

Gradually speeding it up

Metronome Setting	L	R	T	CM
♩=100 1 note per beat	☐	☐	☐	☐
♩=120 1 note per beat	☐	☐	☐	☐
♩=150 1 note per beat	☐	☐	☐	☐
♩=90 2 notes per beat	☐	☐	☐	☐
♩=105 2 notes per beat	☐	☐	☐	☐
♩=120 2 notes per beat	☐	☐	☐	☐
♩=135 2 notes per beat	☐	☐	☐	☐
♩=150 2 notes per beat	☐	☐	☐	☐
♩=80 4 notes per beat	☐	☐	☐	☐
♩=90 4 notes per beat	☐	☐	☐	☐
♩=100 4 notes per beat	☐	☐	☐	☐
♩=110 4 notes per beat	☐	☐	☐	☐
♩=120 4 notes per beat	☐	☐	☐	☐
♩=130 4 notes per beat	☐	☐	☐	☐
♩=140 4 notes per beat	☐	☐	☐	☐

CM is contrary motion. Contrary scales are 2 octaves, all others are 4 octaves. Must be **twice in a row correct**.

Very Easy | **Easy** | Moderate | Challenging | Difficult

D Minor

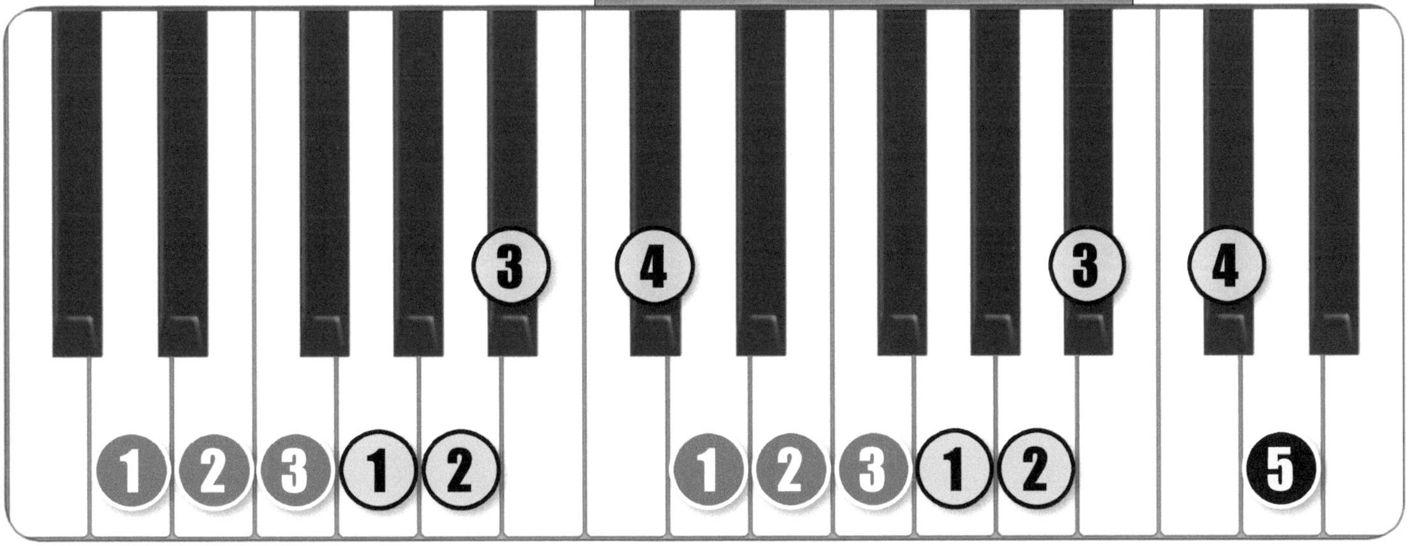

③ Twists

Brain hurtingly tough challenges

		1	2	3	4	5	6	7	8	9	10
Rhythm	**74**	☐	☐	☐	☐	☐	☐	☐	☐	☐	☐
Articulation	**76**	☐	☐	☐	☐	☐	☐	☐	☐	☐	☐
Dynamic	**78**	☐	☐	☐	☐	☐	☐	☐	☐	☐	☐
Ratio	**80**	☐	☐	☐	☐	☐	☐	☐	☐	–	–
Balance	**82**	☐	☐	☐	☐	☐	☐	☐	☐	–	–
Cacophony	**84**	☐	☐	☐	☐	☐	☐	☐	☐	☐	☐
Cascade	**86**	☐	☐	☐	☐	☐	☐	–	–	–	–
Interval	**88**	☐	☐	☐	☐	☐	☐	☐	☐	☐	☐
Contrary	**90**	☐	☐	☐	☐	☐	☐	–	–	–	–

Twists must be completed **2 hands together**

Track your Progress

Count your completed Challenges

1 ○ Dabbling
3 ○ Beginner
8 ○ Apprentice
16 ○ Aspiring
27 ○ Experienced
41 ○ Skilled
58 ○ Proficient
78 ○ Expert
101 ○ Master
127 ○ Grandmaster
156 ○ Legendary
189 ○ Yours for life*

* You'll *never* forget this scale, even if you never practice it again.

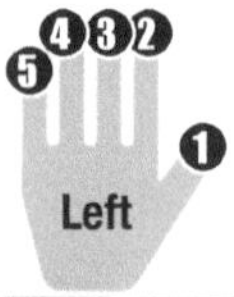

D Major

Very Easy | **Easy** | Moderate | Challenging | Difficult

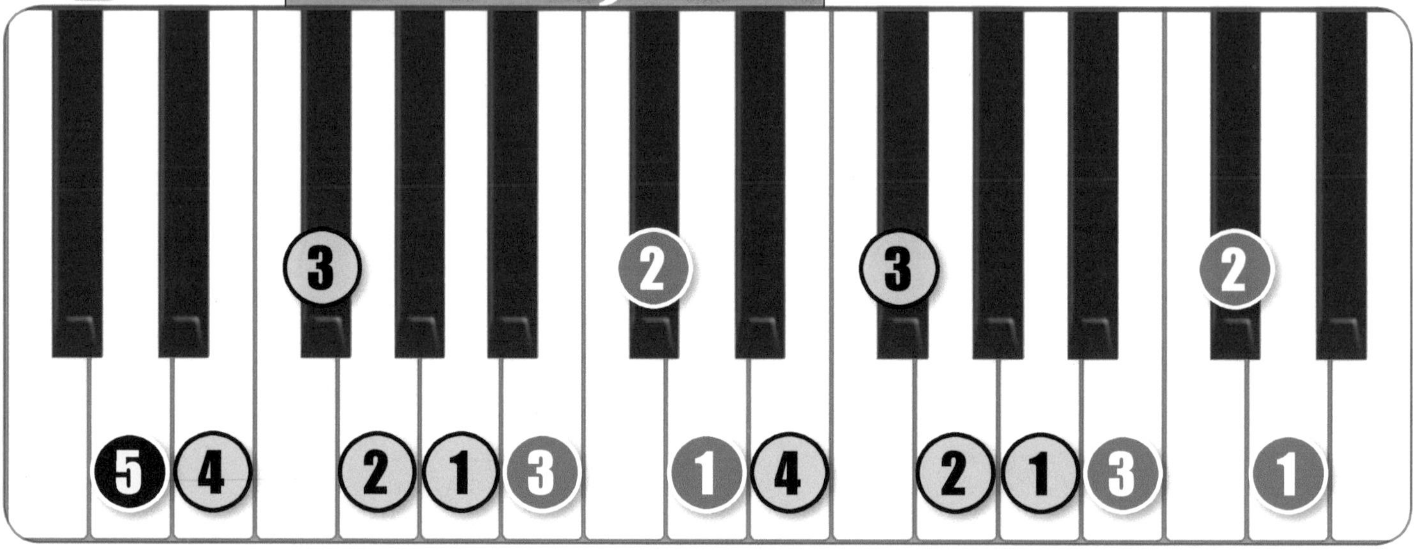

① Core Challenges

Start with these

Page		L	R	T
68	First Playthrough	☐	☐	☐
68	First from Memory	☐	☐	☐
68	First Contrary Motion	–	–	☐
68	4 Octave Tour	☐	☐	☐
69	Grand Tour	☐	☐	☐
69	Thrice is Nice	☐	☐	☐
69	10 in a Row	☐	☐	☐
69	3 Minute Quota	☐	☐	☐
70	3 Minute Tightrope	☐	☐	☐
70	Marathon Tightrope	☐	☐	☐
70	Witnessed by 6	☐	☐	☐
70	Lesson Startup	☐	☐	☐
71	Super Slow Motion	☐	☐	☐
71	Commentator	☐	☐	–
71	Splatmaster	☐	☐	–
72	By Feel Alone	☐	☐	☐
72	Tabletop Scale	☐	☐	☐
72	Repertoire	–	–	☐
72	Octave Collector	☐	☐	☐

L is Left Hand, **R** is Right Hand, **T** is Together

② Tempo Milestones

Gradually speeding it up

Metronome Setting	L	R	T	CM
♩=100 1 note per beat	☐	☐	☐	☐
♩=120 1 note per beat	☐	☐	☐	☐
♩=150 1 note per beat	☐	☐	☐	☐
♩=90 2 notes per beat	☐	☐	☐	☐
♩=105 2 notes per beat	☐	☐	☐	☐
♩=120 2 notes per beat	☐	☐	☐	☐
♩=135 2 notes per beat	☐	☐	☐	☐
♩=150 2 notes per beat	☐	☐	☐	☐
♩=80 4 notes per beat	☐	☐	☐	☐
♩=90 4 notes per beat	☐	☐	☐	☐
♩=100 4 notes per beat	☐	☐	☐	☐
♩=110 4 notes per beat	☐	☐	☐	☐
♩=120 4 notes per beat	☐	☐	☐	☐
♩=130 4 notes per beat	☐	☐	☐	☐
♩=140 4 notes per beat	☐	☐	☐	☐

CM is contrary motion. Contrary scales are 2 octaves, all others are 4 octaves. Must be **twice in a row correct**.

Very Easy | **Easy** | Moderate | Challenging | Difficult

D Major

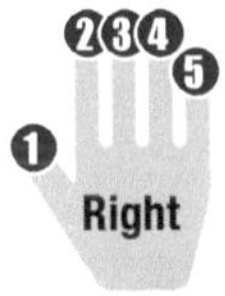

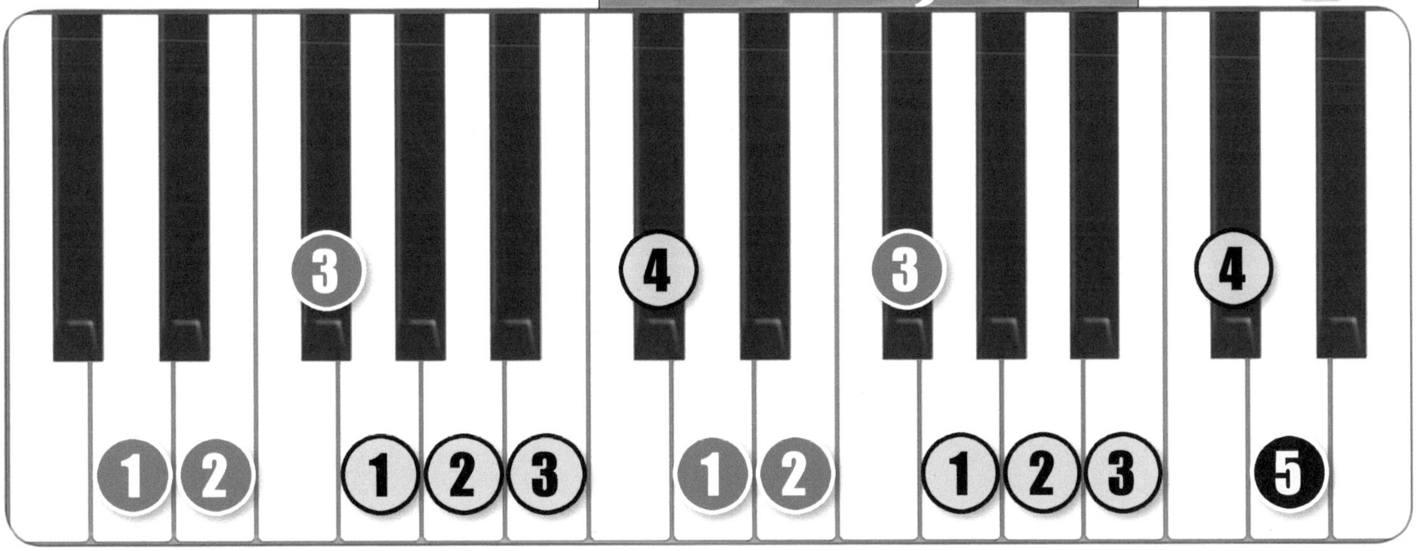

③ Twists

Brain hurtingly tough challenges

		1	2	3	4	5	6	7	8	9	10
Rhythm	**74**	☐	☐	☐	☐	☐	☐	☐	☐	☐	☐
Articulation	**76**	☐	☐	☐	☐	☐	☐	☐	☐	☐	☐
Dynamic	**78**	☐	☐	☐	☐	☐	☐	☐	☐	☐	☐
Ratio	**80**	☐	☐	☐	☐	☐	☐	☐	☐	–	–
Balance	**82**	☐	☐	☐	☐	☐	☐	☐	☐	–	–
Cacophony	**84**	☐	☐	☐	☐	☐	☐	☐	☐	☐	☐
Cascade	**86**	☐	☐	☐	☐	☐	☐	–	–	–	–
Interval	**88**	☐	☐	☐	☐	☐	☐	☐	☐	☐	☐
Contrary	**90**	☐	☐	☐	☐	☐	☐	–	–	–	–

Twists must be completed **2 hands together**

Track your Progress

Count your completed Challenges

- 1 ○ Dabbling
- 3 ○ Beginner
- **8 ○ Apprentice**
- 16 ○ Aspiring
- 27 ○ Experienced
- **41 ○ Skilled**
- 58 ○ Proficient
- 78 ○ Expert
- **101 ○ Master**
- 127 ○ Grandmaster
- 156 ○ Legendary
- **189 ○ Yours for life***

* You'll *never* forget this scale, even if you never practice it again.

Left

D#/Eb Minor

Very Easy | Easy | Moderate | **Challenging** | Difficult

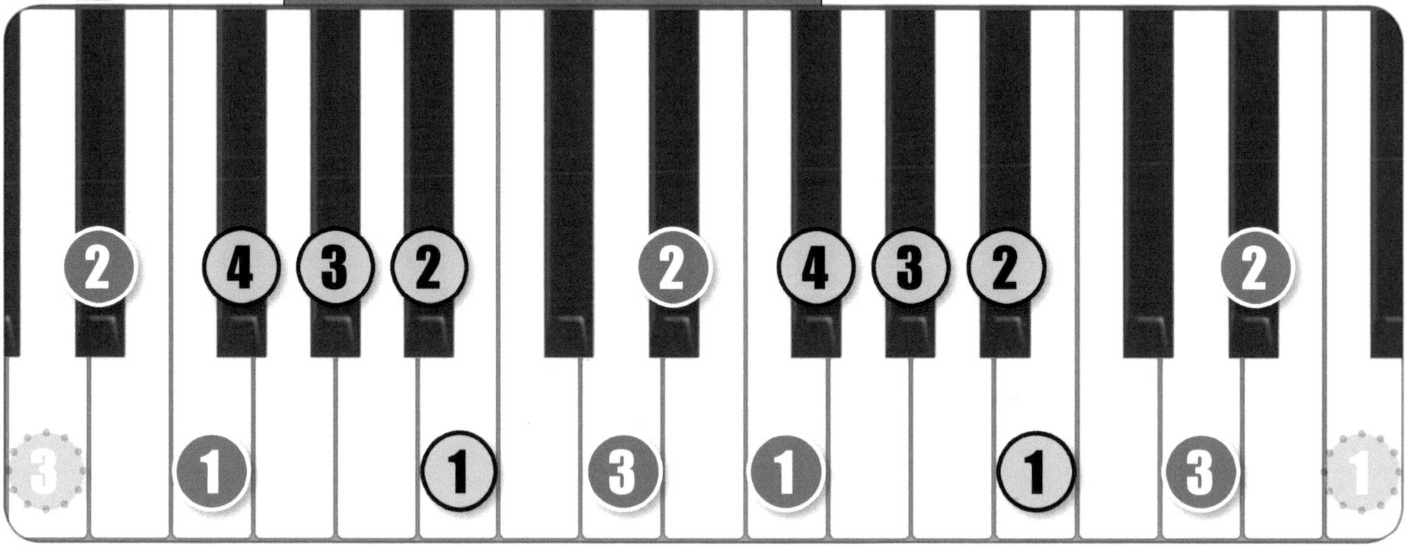

① Core Challenges

Start with these

Page		L	R	T
68	First Playthrough	☐	☐	☐
68	First from Memory	☐	☐	☐
68	First Contrary Motion	–	–	☐
68	4 Octave Tour	☐	☐	☐
69	Grand Tour	☐	☐	☐
69	Thrice is Nice	☐	☐	☐
69	10 in a Row	☐	☐	☐
69	3 Minute Quota	☐	☐	☐
70	3 Minute Tightrope	☐	☐	☐
70	Marathon Tightrope	☐	☐	☐
70	Witnessed by 6	☐	☐	☐
70	Lesson Startup	☐	☐	☐
71	Super Slow Motion	☐	☐	☐
71	Commentator	☐	☐	–
71	Splatmaster	☐	☐	–
72	By Feel Alone	☐	☐	☐
72	Tabletop Scale	☐	☐	☐
72	Repertoire	–	–	☐
72	Octave Collector	☐	☐	☐

L is Left Hand, **R** is Right Hand, **T** is Together

② Tempo Milestones

Gradually speeding it up

Metronome Setting	L	R	T	CM
♩=100 1 note per beat	☐	☐	☐	☐
♩=120 1 note per beat	☐	☐	☐	☐
♩=150 1 note per beat	☐	☐	☐	☐
♩=90 2 notes per beat	☐	☐	☐	☐
♩=105 2 notes per beat	☐	☐	☐	☐
♩=120 2 notes per beat	☐	☐	☐	☐
♩=135 2 notes per beat	☐	☐	☐	☐
♩=150 2 notes per beat	☐	☐	☐	☐
♩=80 4 notes per beat	☐	☐	☐	☐
♩=90 4 notes per beat	☐	☐	☐	☐
♩=100 4 notes per beat	☐	☐	☐	☐
♩=110 4 notes per beat	☐	☐	☐	☐
♩=120 4 notes per beat	☐	☐	☐	☐
♩=130 4 notes per beat	☐	☐	☐	☐
♩=140 4 notes per beat	☐	☐	☐	☐

CM is contrary motion. Contrary scales are 2 octaves, all others are 4 octaves. Must be **twice in a row correct**.

Very Easy | Easy | Moderate | **Challenging** | Difficult

D#/Eb Minor

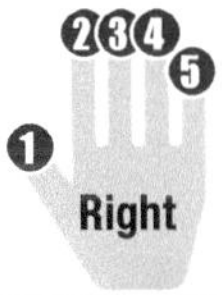

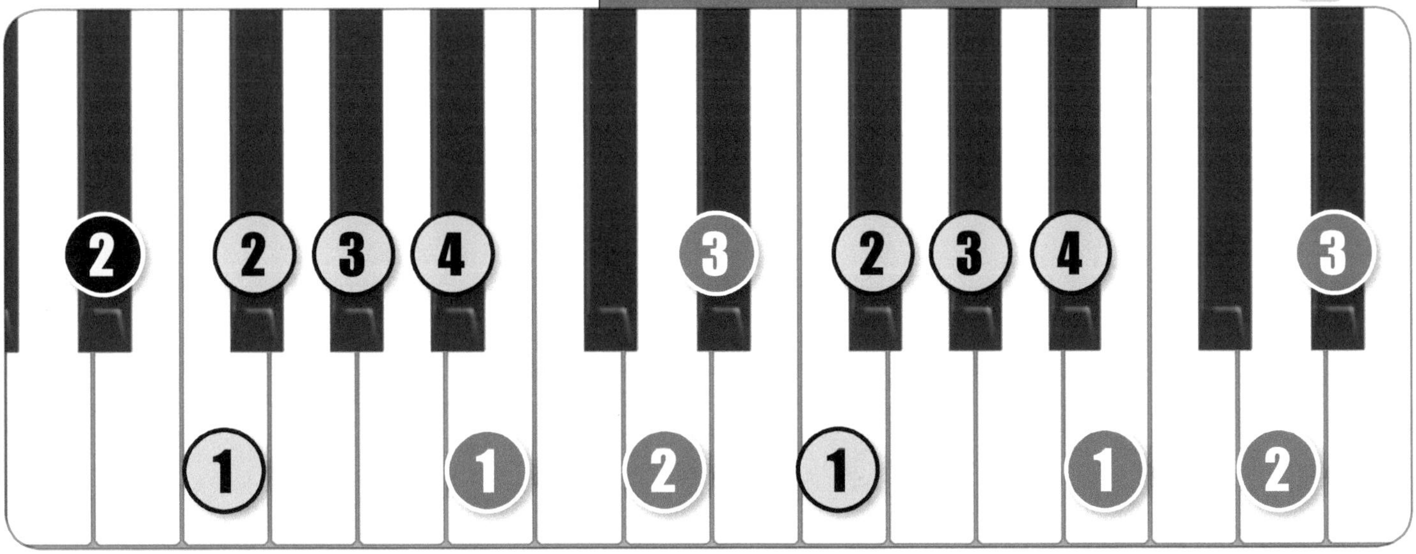

③ Twists

Brain hurtingly tough challenges

		1	2	3	4	5	6	7	8	9	10
Rhythm	**74**	☐	☐	☐	☐	☐	☐	☐	☐	☐	☐
Articulation	**76**	☐	☐	☐	☐	☐	☐	☐	☐	☐	☐
Dynamic	**78**	☐	☐	☐	☐	☐	☐	☐	☐	☐	☐
Ratio	**80**	☐	☐	☐	☐	☐	☐	☐	☐	–	–
Balance	**82**	☐	☐	☐	☐	☐	☐	☐	☐	–	–
Cacophony	**84**	☐	☐	☐	☐	☐	☐	☐	☐	☐	☐
Cascade	**86**	☐	☐	☐	☐	☐	☐	–	–	–	–
Interval	**88**	☐	☐	☐	☐	☐	☐	☐	☐	☐	☐
Contrary	**90**	☐	☐	☐	☐	☐	☐	–	–	–	–

Twists must be completed **2 hands together**

Track your Progress

Count your completed Challenges

- 1 ○ Dabbling
- 3 ○ Beginner
- **8** ○ **Apprentice**
- 16 ○ Aspiring
- 27 ○ Experienced
- **41** ○ **Skilled**
- 58 ○ Proficient
- 78 ○ Expert
- **101** ○ **Master**
- 127 ○ Grandmaster
- 156 ○ Legendary
- **189** ○ **Yours for life***

* You'll *never* forget this scale, even if you never practice it again.

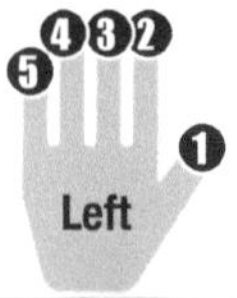

E♭ Major

Very Easy | Easy | **Moderate** | Challenging | Difficult

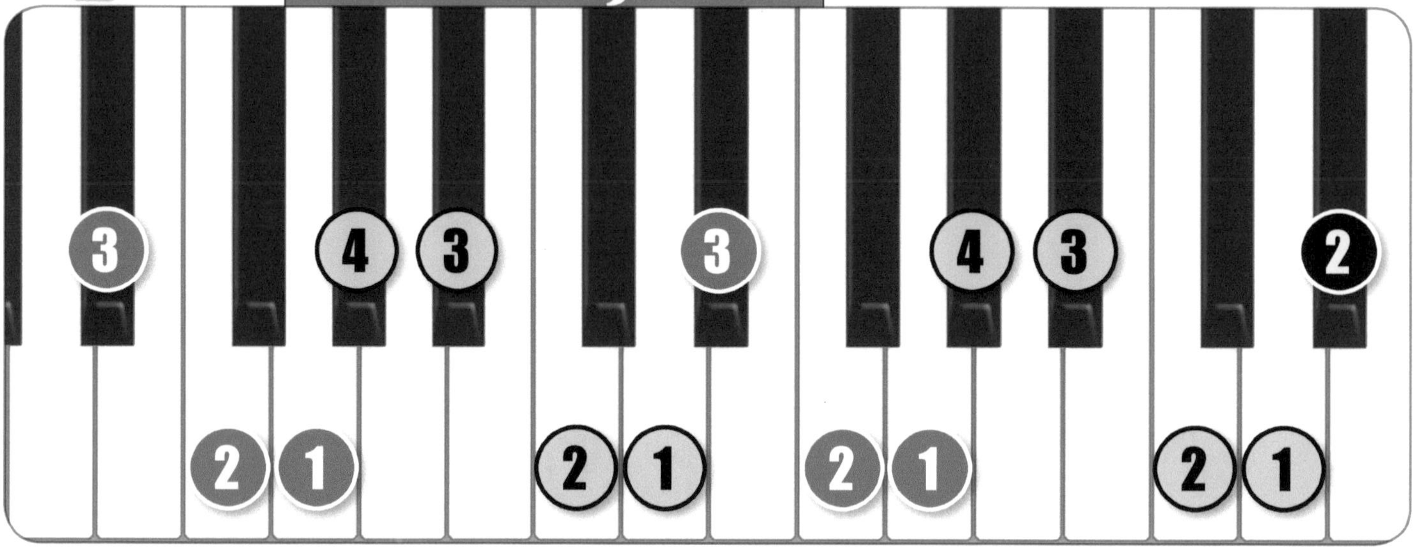

① Core Challenges

Start with these

Page		L	R	T
68	First Playthrough	☐	☐	☐
68	First from Memory	☐	☐	☐
68	First Contrary Motion	—	—	☐
68	4 Octave Tour	☐	☐	☐
69	Grand Tour	☐	☐	☐
69	Thrice is Nice	☐	☐	☐
69	10 in a Row	☐	☐	☐
69	3 Minute Quota	☐	☐	☐
70	3 Minute Tightrope	☐	☐	☐
70	Marathon Tightrope	☐	☐	☐
70	Witnessed by 6	☐	☐	☐
70	Lesson Startup	☐	☐	☐
71	Super Slow Motion	☐	☐	☐
71	Commentator	☐	☐	—
71	Splatmaster	☐	☐	—
72	By Feel Alone	☐	☐	☐
72	Tabletop Scale	☐	☐	☐
72	Repertoire	—	—	☐
72	Octave Collector	☐	☐	☐

L is Left Hand, **R** is Right Hand, **T** is Together

② Tempo Milestones

Gradually speeding it up

Metronome Setting	L	R	T	CM
♩=100 1 note per beat	☐	☐	☐	☐
♩=120 1 note per beat	☐	☐	☐	☐
♩=150 1 note per beat	☐	☐	☐	☐
♩=90 2 notes per beat	☐	☐	☐	☐
♩=105 2 notes per beat	☐	☐	☐	☐
♩=120 2 notes per beat	☐	☐	☐	☐
♩=135 2 notes per beat	☐	☐	☐	☐
♩=150 2 notes per beat	☐	☐	☐	☐
♩=80 4 notes per beat	☐	☐	☐	☐
♩=90 4 notes per beat	☐	☐	☐	☐
♩=100 4 notes per beat	☐	☐	☐	☐
♩=110 4 notes per beat	☐	☐	☐	☐
♩=120 4 notes per beat	☐	☐	☐	☐
♩=130 4 notes per beat	☐	☐	☐	☐
♩=140 4 notes per beat	☐	☐	☐	☐

CM is contrary motion. Contrary scales are 2 octaves, all others are 4 octaves. Must be **twice in a row correct**.

Very Easy | Easy | **Moderate** | Challenging | Difficult

E♭ Major

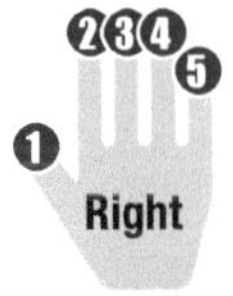

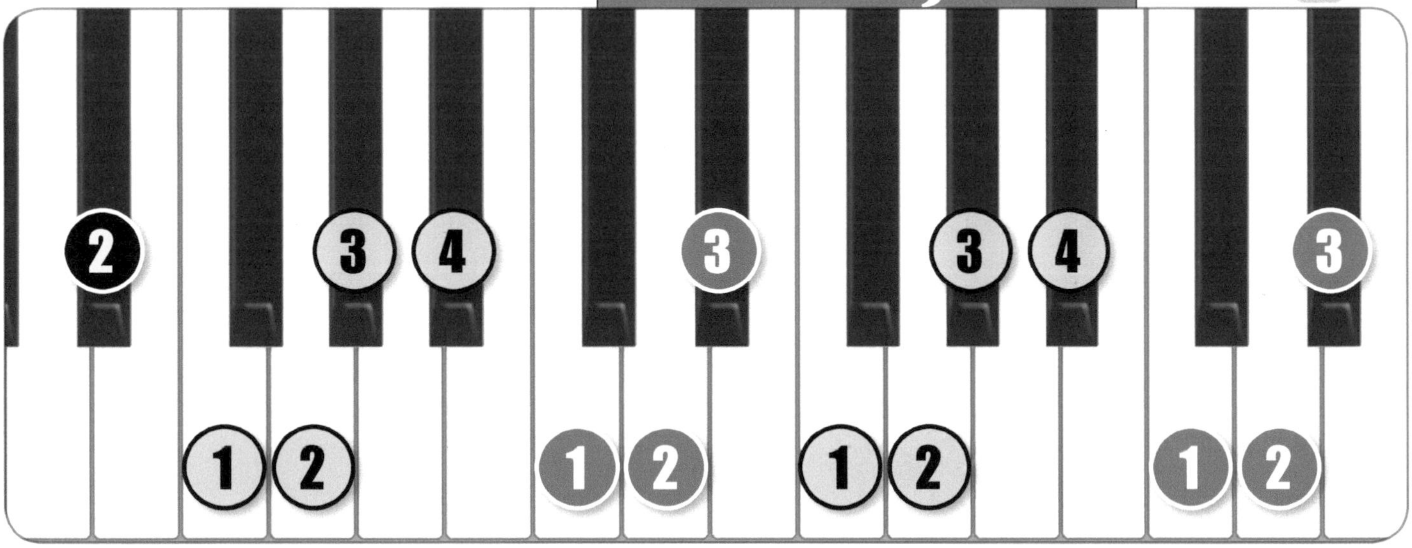

③ Twists

Brain hurtingly tough challenges

		1	2	3	4	5	6	7	8	9	10
Rhythm	**74**	☐	☐	☐	☐	☐	☐	☐	☐	☐	☐
Articulation	**76**	☐	☐	☐	☐	☐	☐	☐	☐	☐	☐
Dynamic	**78**	☐	☐	☐	☐	☐	☐	☐	☐	☐	☐
Ratio	**80**	☐	☐	☐	☐	☐	☐	☐	☐	–	–
Balance	**82**	☐	☐	☐	☐	☐	☐	☐	☐	–	–
Cacophony	**84**	☐	☐	☐	☐	☐	☐	☐	☐	☐	☐
Cascade	**86**	☐	☐	☐	☐	☐	☐	–	–	–	–
Interval	**88**	☐	☐	☐	☐	☐	☐	☐	☐	☐	☐
Contrary	**90**	☐	☐	☐	☐	☐	☐	–	–	–	–

Twists must be completed **2 hands together**

Track your Progress

Count your completed Challenges

- 1 ○ Dabbling
- 3 ○ Beginner
- **8 ○ Apprentice**
- 16 ○ Aspiring
- 27 ○ Experienced
- **41 ○ Skilled**
- 58 ○ Proficient
- 78 ○ Expert
- **101 ○ Master**
- 127 ○ Grandmaster
- 156 ○ Legendary
- **189 ○ Yours for life***

* You'll *never* forget this scale,
even if you never practice it again.

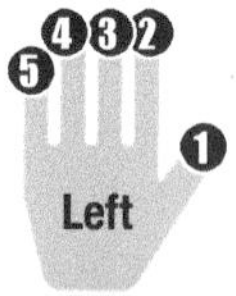

E Minor

Very Easy | **Easy** | Moderate | Challenging | Difficult

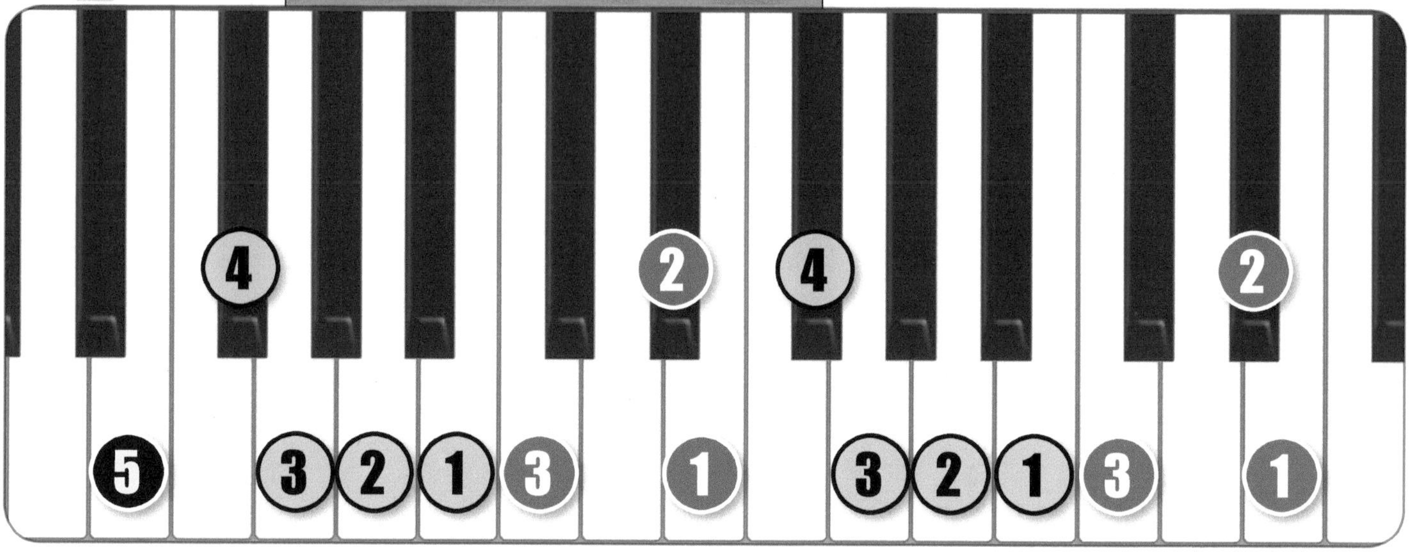

① Core Challenges

Start with these

Page		L	R	T
68	First Playthrough	☐	☐	☐
68	First from Memory	☐	☐	☐
68	First Contrary Motion	—	—	☐
68	4 Octave Tour	☐	☐	☐
69	Grand Tour	☐	☐	☐
69	Thrice is Nice	☐	☐	☐
69	10 in a Row	☐	☐	☐
69	3 Minute Quota	☐	☐	☐
70	3 Minute Tightrope	☐	☐	☐
70	Marathon Tightrope	☐	☐	☐
70	Witnessed by 6	☐	☐	☐
70	Lesson Startup	☐	☐	☐
71	Super Slow Motion	☐	☐	☐
71	Commentator	☐	☐	—
71	Splatmaster	☐	☐	—
72	By Feel Alone	☐	☐	☐
72	Tabletop Scale	☐	☐	☐
72	Repertoire	—	—	☐
72	Octave Collector	☐	☐	☐

L is Left Hand, **R** is Right Hand, **T** is Together

② Tempo Milestones

Gradually speeding it up

Metronome Setting	L	R	T	CM
♩=100 1 note per beat	☐	☐	☐	☐
♩=120 1 note per beat	☐	☐	☐	☐
♩=150 1 note per beat	☐	☐	☐	☐
♩=90 2 notes per beat	☐	☐	☐	☐
♩=105 2 notes per beat	☐	☐	☐	☐
♩=120 2 notes per beat	☐	☐	☐	☐
♩=135 2 notes per beat	☐	☐	☐	☐
♩=150 2 notes per beat	☐	☐	☐	☐
♩=80 4 notes per beat	☐	☐	☐	☐
♩=90 4 notes per beat	☐	☐	☐	☐
♩=100 4 notes per beat	☐	☐	☐	☐
♩=110 4 notes per beat	☐	☐	☐	☐
♩=120 4 notes per beat	☐	☐	☐	☐
♩=130 4 notes per beat	☐	☐	☐	☐
♩=140 4 notes per beat	☐	☐	☐	☐

CM is contrary motion. Contrary scales are 2 octaves, all others are 4 octaves. Must be **twice in a row correct**.

Very Easy | **Easy** | Moderate | Challenging | Difficult

E Minor

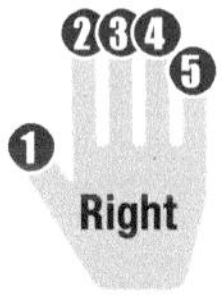

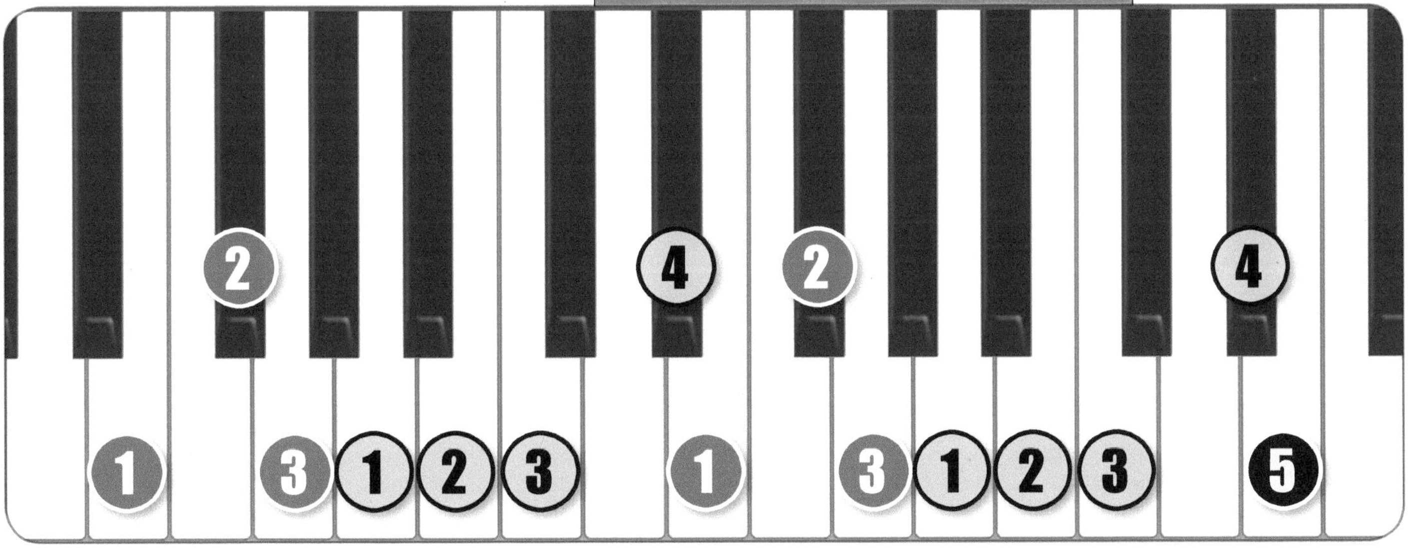

③ Twists

Brain hurtingly tough challenges

		1	2	3	4	5	6	7	8	9	10
Rhythm	**74**	☐	☐	☐	☐	☐	☐	☐	☐	☐	☐
Articulation	**76**	☐	☐	☐	☐	☐	☐	☐	☐	☐	☐
Dynamic	**78**	☐	☐	☐	☐	☐	☐	☐	☐	☐	☐
Ratio	**80**	☐	☐	☐	☐	☐	☐	☐	☐	–	–
Balance	**82**	☐	☐	☐	☐	☐	☐	☐	☐	–	–
Cacophony	**84**	☐	☐	☐	☐	☐	☐	☐	☐	☐	☐
Cascade	**86**	☐	☐	☐	☐	☐	☐	–	–	–	–
Interval	**88**	☐	☐	☐	☐	☐	☐	☐	☐	☐	☐
Contrary	**90**	☐	☐	☐	☐	☐	☐	–	–	–	–

Twists must be completed **2 hands together**

Track your Progress

Count your completed Challenges

- 1 ○ Dabbling
- 3 ○ Beginner
- **8 ○ Apprentice**
- 16 ○ Aspiring
- 27 ○ Experienced
- **41 ○ Skilled**
- 58 ○ Proficient
- 78 ○ Expert
- **101 ○ Master**
- 127 ○ Grandmaster
- 156 ○ Legendary
- **189 ○ Yours for life***

* You'll ***never*** forget this scale, even if you never practice it again.

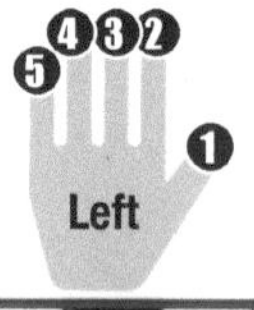

E Major

Very Easy | **Easy** | Moderate | Challenging | Difficult

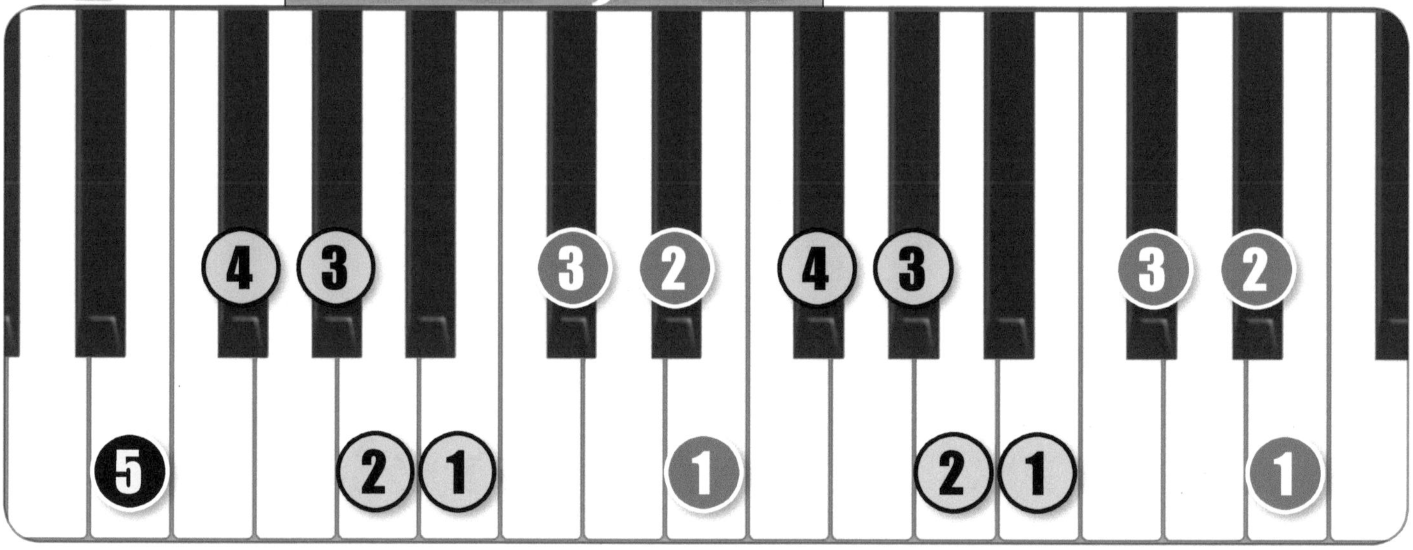

① Core Challenges

Start with these

Page		L	R	T
68	First Playthrough	☐	☐	☐
68	First from Memory	☐	☐	☐
68	First Contrary Motion	–	–	☐
68	4 Octave Tour	☐	☐	☐
69	Grand Tour	☐	☐	☐
69	Thrice is Nice	☐	☐	☐
69	10 in a Row	☐	☐	☐
69	3 Minute Quota	☐	☐	☐
70	3 Minute Tightrope	☐	☐	☐
70	Marathon Tightrope	☐	☐	☐
70	Witnessed by 6	☐	☐	☐
70	Lesson Startup	☐	☐	☐
71	Super Slow Motion	☐	☐	☐
71	Commentator	☐	☐	–
71	Splatmaster	☐	☐	–
72	By Feel Alone	☐	☐	☐
72	Tabletop Scale	☐	☐	☐
72	Repertoire	–	–	☐
72	Octave Collector	☐	☐	☐

L is Left Hand, **R** is Right Hand, **T** is Together

② Tempo Milestones

Gradually speeding it up

Metronome Setting	L	R	T	CM
♩=100 1 note per beat	☐	☐	☐	☐
♩=120 1 note per beat	☐	☐	☐	☐
♩=150 1 note per beat	☐	☐	☐	☐
♩=90 2 notes per beat	☐	☐	☐	☐
♩=105 2 notes per beat	☐	☐	☐	☐
♩=120 2 notes per beat	☐	☐	☐	☐
♩=135 2 notes per beat	☐	☐	☐	☐
♩=150 2 notes per beat	☐	☐	☐	☐
♩=80 4 notes per beat	☐	☐	☐	☐
♩=90 4 notes per beat	☐	☐	☐	☐
♩=100 4 notes per beat	☐	☐	☐	☐
♩=110 4 notes per beat	☐	☐	☐	☐
♩=120 4 notes per beat	☐	☐	☐	☐
♩=130 4 notes per beat	☐	☐	☐	☐
♩=140 4 notes per beat	☐	☐	☐	☐

CM is contrary motion. Contrary scales are 2 octaves, all others are 4 octaves. Must be **twice in a row correct**.

Very Easy | **Easy** | Moderate | Challenging | Difficult

E Major

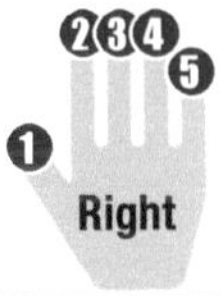

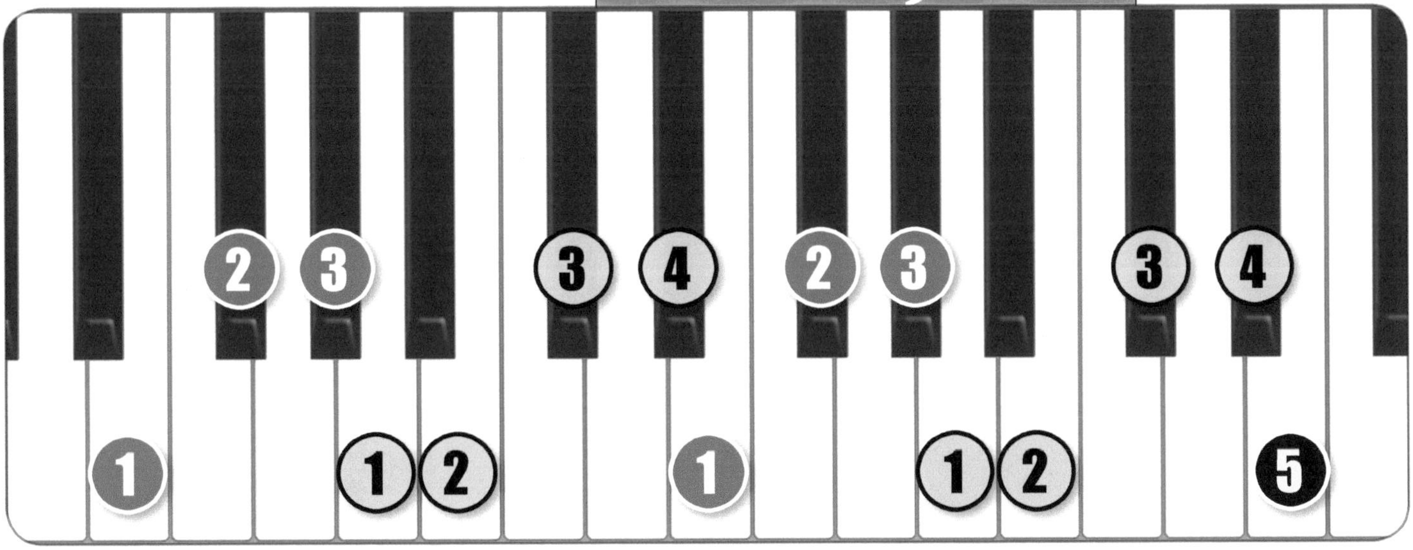

③ Twists

Brain hurtingly tough challenges

		1	2	3	4	5	6	7	8	9	10
Rhythm	**74**	☐	☐	☐	☐	☐	☐	☐	☐	☐	☐
Articulation	**76**	☐	☐	☐	☐	☐	☐	☐	☐	☐	☐
Dynamic	**78**	☐	☐	☐	☐	☐	☐	☐	☐	☐	☐
Ratio	**80**	☐	☐	☐	☐	☐	☐	☐	☐	–	–
Balance	**82**	☐	☐	☐	☐	☐	☐	☐	☐	–	–
Cacophony	**84**	☐	☐	☐	☐	☐	☐	☐	☐	☐	☐
Cascade	**86**	☐	☐	☐	☐	☐	☐	–	–	–	–
Interval	**88**	☐	☐	☐	☐	☐	☐	☐	☐	☐	☐
Contrary	**90**	☐	☐	☐	☐	☐	☐	–	–	–	–

Twists must be completed **2 hands together**

Track your Progress

Count your completed Challenges

1 ○ Dabbling
3 ○ Beginner
8 ○ Apprentice
16 ○ Aspiring
27 ○ Experienced
41 ○ Skilled
58 ○ Proficient
78 ○ Expert
101 ○ Master
127 ○ Grandmaster
156 ○ Legendary
189 ○ Yours for life*

* You'll *never* forget this scale, even if you never practice it again.

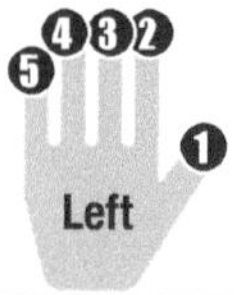

F Minor

Very Easy | Easy | **Moderate** | Challenging | Difficult

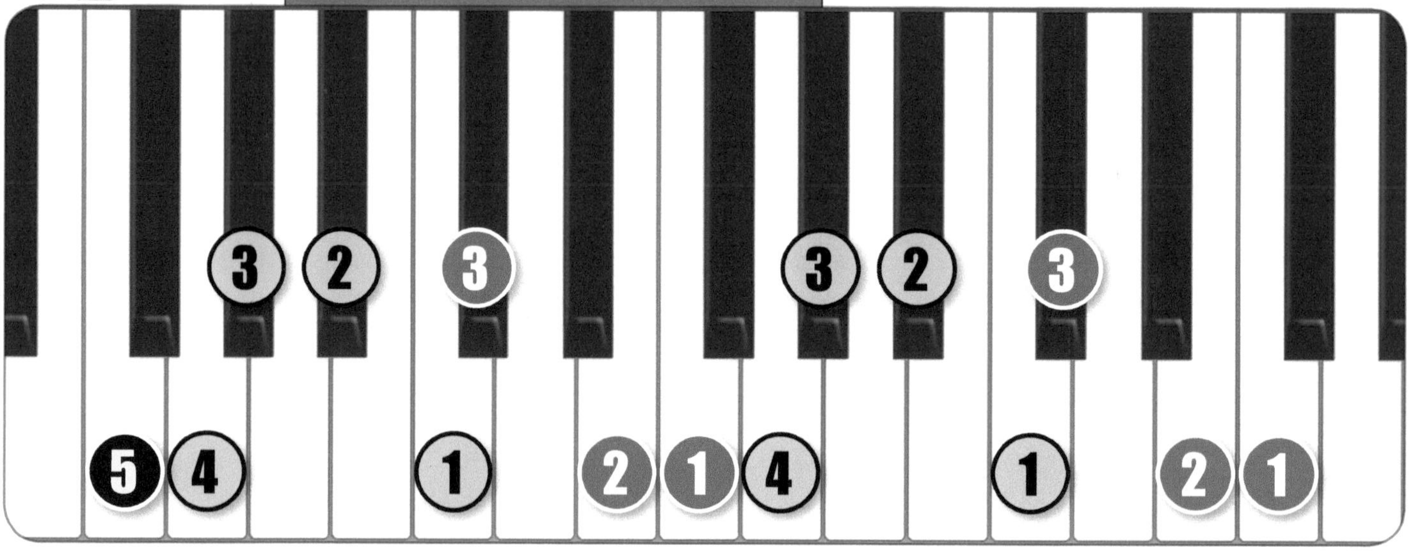

① Core Challenges

Start with these

Page		L	R	T
68	First Playthrough	☐	☐	☐
68	First from Memory	☐	☐	☐
68	First Contrary Motion	—	—	☐
68	4 Octave Tour	☐	☐	☐
69	Grand Tour	☐	☐	☐
69	Thrice is Nice	☐	☐	☐
69	10 in a Row	☐	☐	☐
69	3 Minute Quota	☐	☐	☐
70	3 Minute Tightrope	☐	☐	☐
70	Marathon Tightrope	☐	☐	☐
70	Witnessed by 6	☐	☐	☐
70	Lesson Startup	☐	☐	☐
71	Super Slow Motion	☐	☐	☐
71	Commentator	☐	☐	—
71	Splatmaster	☐	☐	—
72	By Feel Alone	☐	☐	☐
72	Tabletop Scale	☐	☐	☐
72	Repertoire	—	—	☐
72	Octave Collector	☐	☐	☐

L is Left Hand, **R** is Right Hand, **T** is Together

② Tempo Milestones

Gradually speeding it up

Metronome Setting	L	R	T	CM
♩=100 1 note per beat	☐	☐	☐	☐
♩=120 1 note per beat	☐	☐	☐	☐
♩=150 1 note per beat	☐	☐	☐	☐
♩=90 2 notes per beat	☐	☐	☐	☐
♩=105 2 notes per beat	☐	☐	☐	☐
♩=120 2 notes per beat	☐	☐	☐	☐
♩=135 2 notes per beat	☐	☐	☐	☐
♩=150 2 notes per beat	☐	☐	☐	☐
♩=80 4 notes per beat	☐	☐	☐	☐
♩=90 4 notes per beat	☐	☐	☐	☐
♩=100 4 notes per beat	☐	☐	☐	☐
♩=110 4 notes per beat	☐	☐	☐	☐
♩=120 4 notes per beat	☐	☐	☐	☐
♩=130 4 notes per beat	☐	☐	☐	☐
♩=140 4 notes per beat	☐	☐	☐	☐

CM is contrary motion. Contrary scales are 2 octaves, all others are 4 octaves. Must be **twice in a row correct**.

Very Easy | Easy | **Moderate** | Challenging | Difficult

F Minor

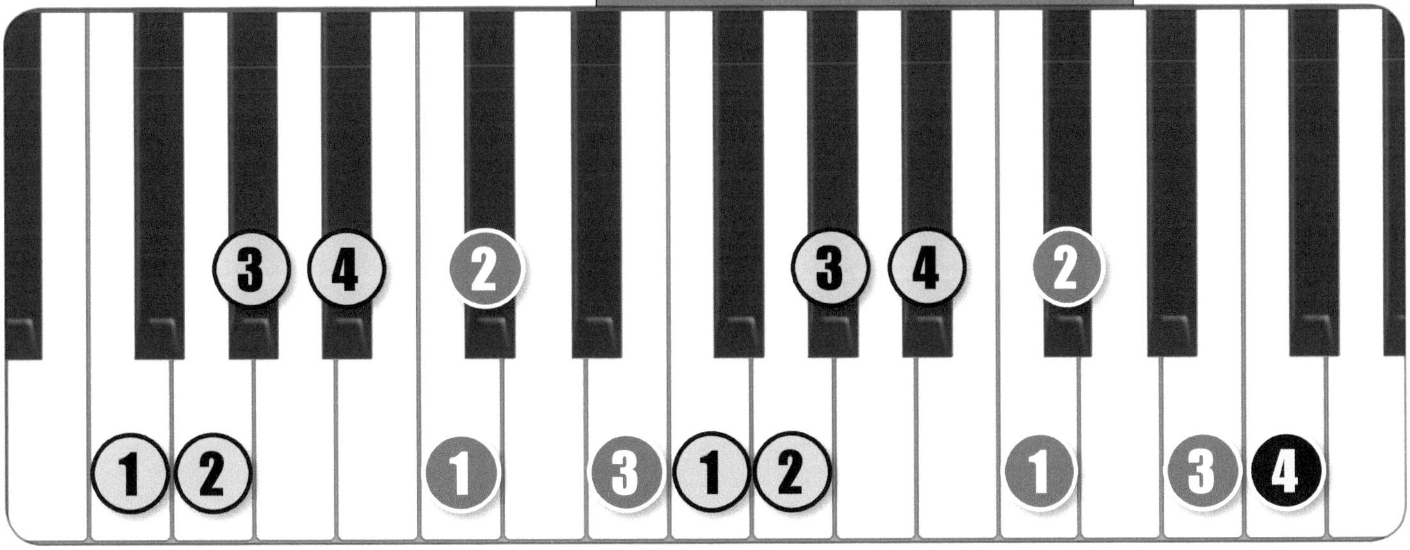

③ Twists

Brain hurtingly tough challenges

		1	2	3	4	5	6	7	8	9	10
Rhythm	**74**	☐	☐	☐	☐	☐	☐	☐	☐	☐	☐
Articulation	**76**	☐	☐	☐	☐	☐	☐	☐	☐	☐	☐
Dynamic	**78**	☐	☐	☐	☐	☐	☐	☐	☐	☐	☐
Ratio	**80**	☐	☐	☐	☐	☐	☐	☐	☐	–	–
Balance	**82**	☐	☐	☐	☐	☐	☐	☐	☐	–	–
Cacophony	**84**	☐	☐	☐	☐	☐	☐	☐	☐	☐	☐
Cascade	**86**	☐	☐	☐	☐	☐	☐	–	–	–	–
Interval	**88**	☐	☐	☐	☐	☐	☐	☐	☐	☐	☐
Contrary	**90**	☐	☐	☐	☐	☐	☐	–	–	–	–

Twists must be completed **2 hands together**

Track your Progress

Count your completed Challenges

- 1 ○ Dabbling
- 3 ○ Beginner
- **8 ○ Apprentice**
- 16 ○ Aspiring
- 27 ○ Experienced
- **41 ○ Skilled**
- 58 ○ Proficient
- 78 ○ Expert
- **101 ○ Master**
- 127 ○ Grandmaster
- 156 ○ Legendary
- **189 ○ Yours for life***

* You'll *never* forget this scale, even if you never practice it again.

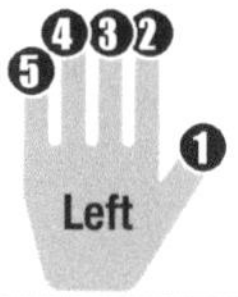

F Major

Very Easy | **Easy** | Moderate | Challenging | Difficult

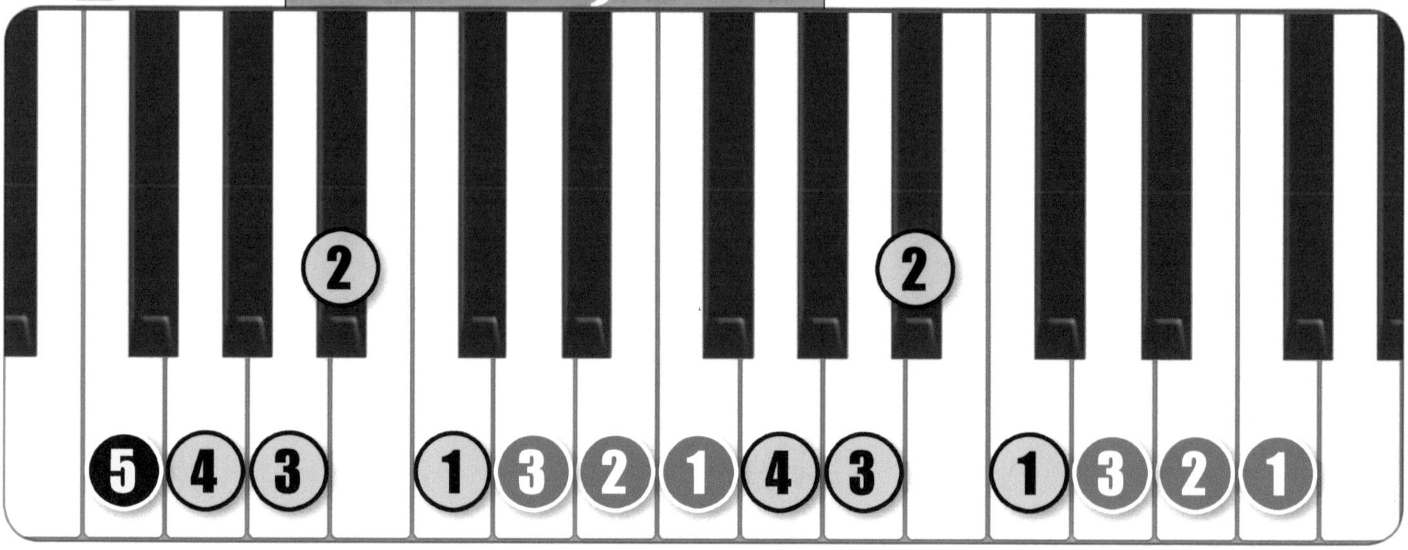

① Core Challenges

Start with these

Page		L	R	T
68	First Playthrough	☐	☐	☐
68	First from Memory	☐	☐	☐
68	First Contrary Motion	–	–	☐
68	4 Octave Tour	☐	☐	☐
69	Grand Tour	☐	☐	☐
69	Thrice is Nice	☐	☐	☐
69	10 in a Row	☐	☐	☐
69	3 Minute Quota	☐	☐	☐
70	3 Minute Tightrope	☐	☐	☐
70	Marathon Tightrope	☐	☐	☐
70	Witnessed by 6	☐	☐	☐
70	Lesson Startup	☐	☐	☐
71	Super Slow Motion	☐	☐	☐
71	Commentator	☐	☐	–
71	Splatmaster	☐	☐	–
72	By Feel Alone	☐	☐	☐
72	Tabletop Scale	☐	☐	☐
72	Repertoire	–	–	☐
72	Octave Collector	☐	☐	☐

L is Left Hand, **R** is Right Hand, **T** is Together

② Tempo Milestones

Gradually speeding it up

Metronome Setting	L	R	T	CM
♩=100 1 note per beat	☐	☐	☐	☐
♩=120 1 note per beat	☐	☐	☐	☐
♩=150 1 note per beat	☐	☐	☐	☐
♩=90 2 notes per beat	☐	☐	☐	☐
♩=105 2 notes per beat	☐	☐	☐	☐
♩=120 2 notes per beat	☐	☐	☐	☐
♩=135 2 notes per beat	☐	☐	☐	☐
♩=150 2 notes per beat	☐	☐	☐	☐
♩=80 4 notes per beat	☐	☐	☐	☐
♩=90 4 notes per beat	☐	☐	☐	☐
♩=100 4 notes per beat	☐	☐	☐	☐
♩=110 4 notes per beat	☐	☐	☐	☐
♩=120 4 notes per beat	☐	☐	☐	☐
♩=130 4 notes per beat	☐	☐	☐	☐
♩=140 4 notes per beat	☐	☐	☐	☐

CM is contrary motion. Contrary scales are 2 octaves, all others are 4 octaves. Must be **twice in a row correct**.

Very Easy | **Easy** | Moderate | Challenging | Difficult

F Major

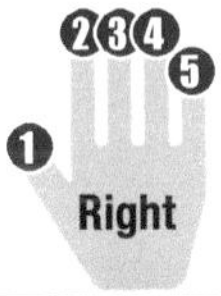

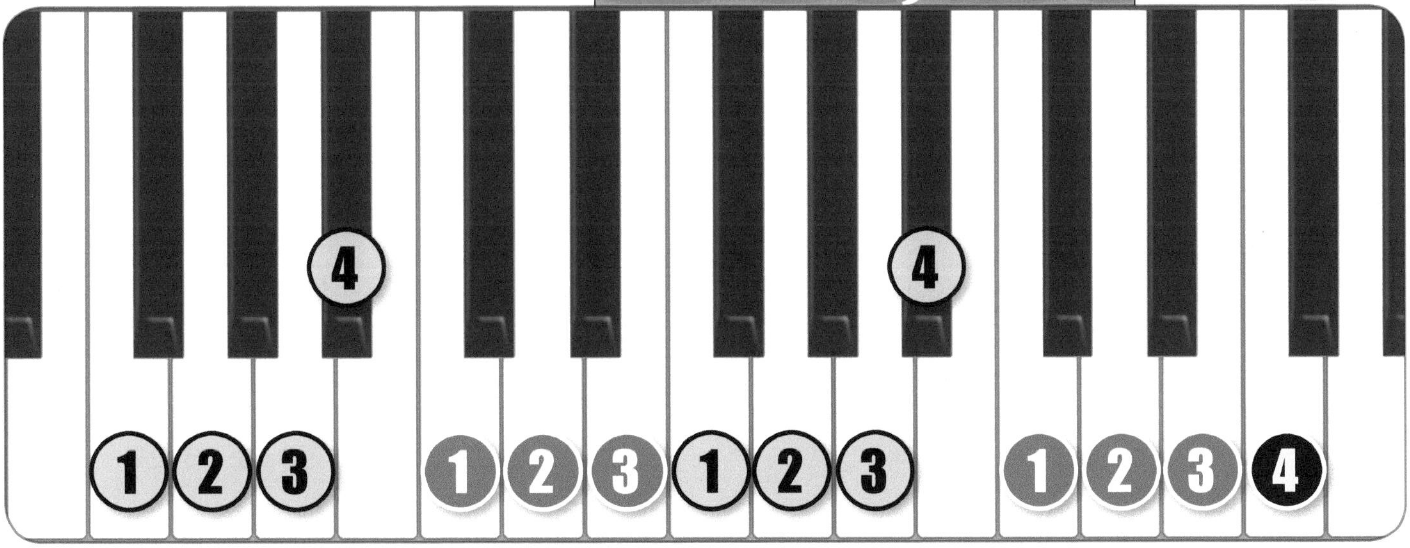

③ Twists

Brain hurtingly tough challenges

		1	2	3	4	5	6	7	8	9	10
Rhythm	**74**	☐	☐	☐	☐	☐	☐	☐	☐	☐	☐
Articulation	**76**	☐	☐	☐	☐	☐	☐	☐	☐	☐	☐
Dynamic	**78**	☐	☐	☐	☐	☐	☐	☐	☐	☐	☐
Ratio	**80**	☐	☐	☐	☐	☐	☐	☐	☐	–	–
Balance	**82**	☐	☐	☐	☐	☐	☐	☐	☐	–	–
Cacophony	**84**	☐	☐	☐	☐	☐	☐	☐	☐	☐	☐
Cascade	**86**	☐	☐	☐	☐	☐	☐	–	–	–	–
Interval	**88**	☐	☐	☐	☐	☐	☐	☐	☐	☐	☐
Contrary	**90**	☐	☐	☐	☐	☐	☐	–	–	–	–

Twists must be completed **2 hands together**

Track your Progress

Count your completed Challenges

- 1 ○ Dabbling
- 3 ○ Beginner
- **8 ○ Apprentice**
- 16 ○ Aspiring
- 27 ○ Experienced
- **41 ○ Skilled**
- 58 ○ Proficient
- 78 ○ Expert
- **101 ○ Master**
- 127 ○ Grandmaster
- 156 ○ Legendary
- **189 ○ Yours for life***

* You'll *never* forget this scale, even if you never practice it again.

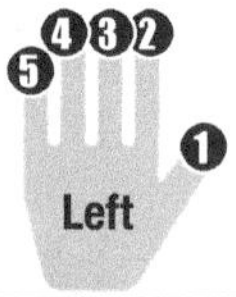

F# Minor

Very Easy | Easy | Moderate | Challenging | **Difficult**

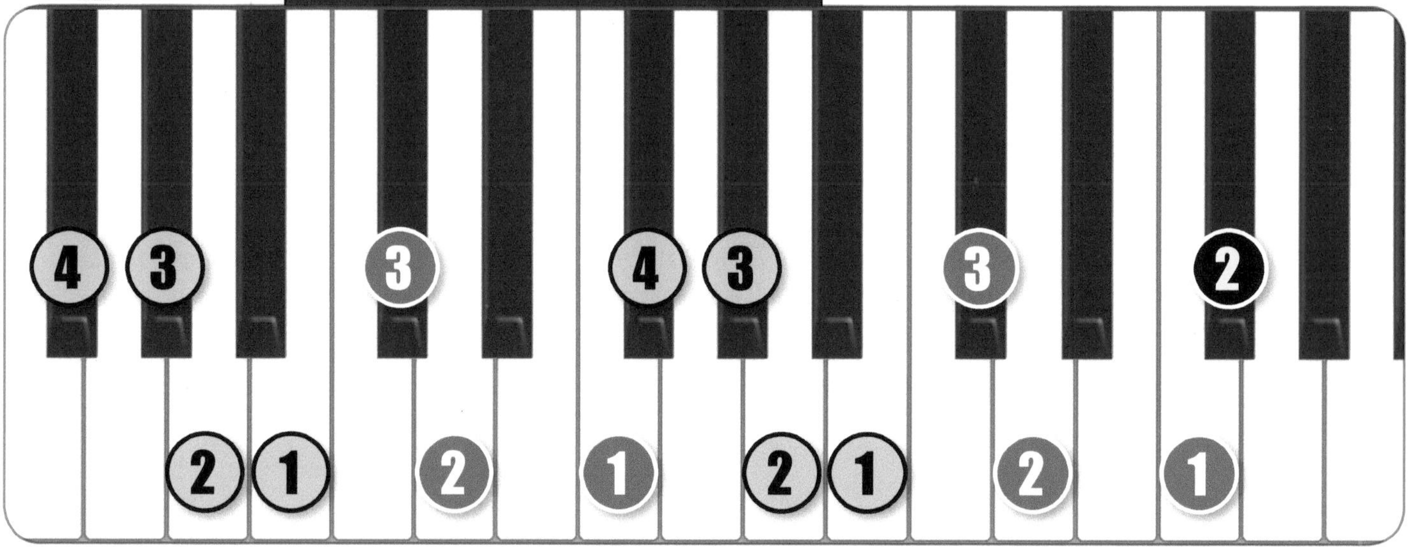

① Core Challenges

Start with these

Page		L	R	T
68	First Playthrough	☐	☐	☐
68	First from Memory	☐	☐	☐
68	First Contrary Motion	—	—	☐
68	4 Octave Tour	☐	☐	☐
69	Grand Tour	☐	☐	☐
69	Thrice is Nice	☐	☐	☐
69	10 in a Row	☐	☐	☐
69	3 Minute Quota	☐	☐	☐
70	3 Minute Tightrope	☐	☐	☐
70	Marathon Tightrope	☐	☐	☐
70	Witnessed by 6	☐	☐	☐
70	Lesson Startup	☐	☐	☐
71	Super Slow Motion	☐	☐	☐
71	Commentator	☐	☐	—
71	Splatmaster	☐	☐	—
72	By Feel Alone	☐	☐	☐
72	Tabletop Scale	☐	☐	☐
72	Repertoire	—	—	☐
72	Octave Collector	☐	☐	☐

L is Left Hand, **R** is Right Hand, **T** is Together

② Tempo Milestones

Gradually speeding it up

Metronome Setting	L	R	T	CM
♩=100 1 note per beat	☐	☐	☐	☐
♩=120 1 note per beat	☐	☐	☐	☐
♩=150 1 note per beat	☐	☐	☐	☐
♩=90 2 notes per beat	☐	☐	☐	☐
♩=105 2 notes per beat	☐	☐	☐	☐
♩=120 2 notes per beat	☐	☐	☐	☐
♩=135 2 notes per beat	☐	☐	☐	☐
♩=150 2 notes per beat	☐	☐	☐	☐
♩=80 4 notes per beat	☐	☐	☐	☐
♩=90 4 notes per beat	☐	☐	☐	☐
♩=100 4 notes per beat	☐	☐	☐	☐
♩=110 4 notes per beat	☐	☐	☐	☐
♩=120 4 notes per beat	☐	☐	☐	☐
♩=130 4 notes per beat	☐	☐	☐	☐
♩=140 4 notes per beat	☐	☐	☐	☐

CM is contrary motion. Contrary scales are 2 octaves, all others are 4 octaves. Must be **twice in a row correct**.

Very Easy | Easy | Moderate | Challenging | **Difficult**

F♯ Minor

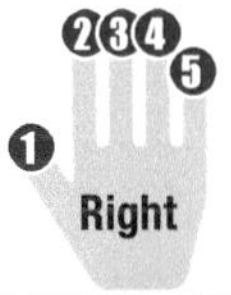

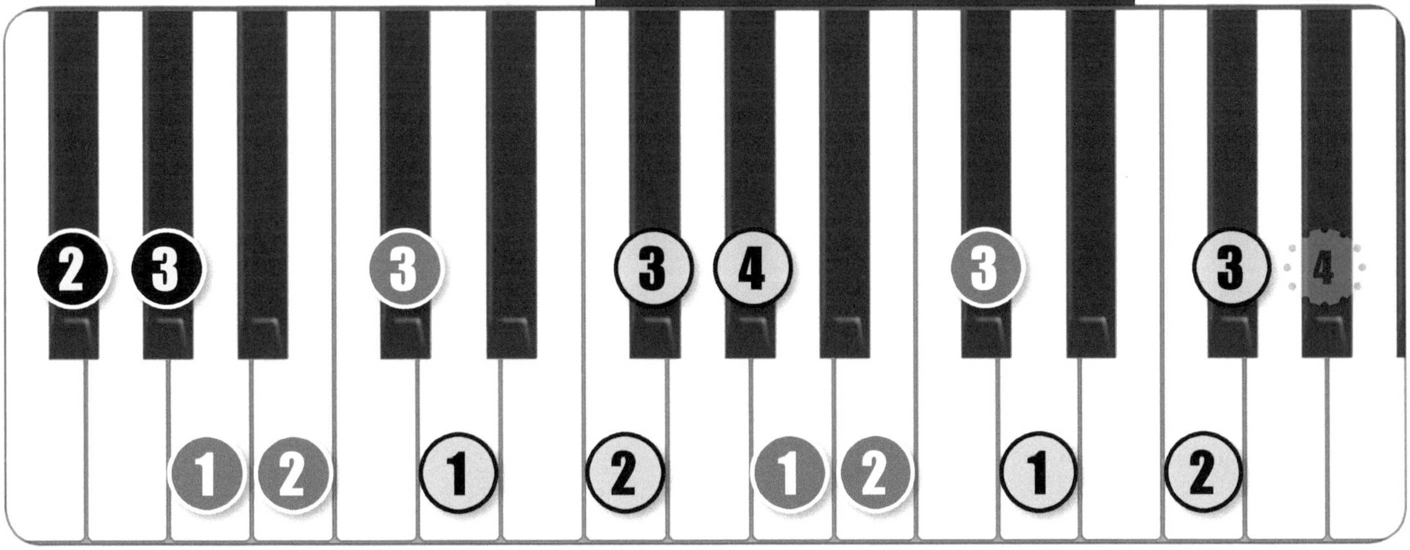

③ Twists

Brain hurtingly tough challenges

		1	2	3	4	5	6	7	8	9	10
Rhythm	**74**	☐	☐	☐	☐	☐	☐	☐	☐	☐	☐
Articulation	**76**	☐	☐	☐	☐	☐	☐	☐	☐	☐	☐
Dynamic	**78**	☐	☐	☐	☐	☐	☐	☐	☐	☐	☐
Ratio	**80**	☐	☐	☐	☐	☐	☐	☐	☐	–	–
Balance	**82**	☐	☐	☐	☐	☐	☐	☐	☐	–	–
Cacophony	**84**	☐	☐	☐	☐	☐	☐	☐	☐	☐	☐
Cascade	**86**	☐	☐	☐	☐	☐	☐	–	–	–	–
Interval	**88**	☐	☐	☐	☐	☐	☐	☐	☐	☐	☐
Contrary	**90**	☐	☐	☐	☐	☐	☐	–	–	–	–

Twists must be completed **2 hands together**

Track your Progress

Count your completed Challenges

- 1 ○ Dabbling
- 3 ○ Beginner
- **8 ○ Apprentice**
- 16 ○ Aspiring
- 27 ○ Experienced
- **41 ○ Skilled**
- 58 ○ Proficient
- 78 ○ Expert
- **101 ○ Master**
- 127 ○ Grandmaster
- 156 ○ Legendary
- **189 ○ Yours for life***

* You'll *never* forget this scale, even if you never practice it again.

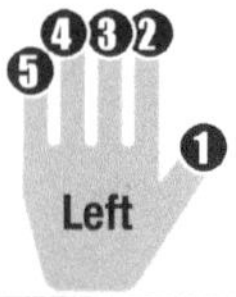

F#/Gb Major

Very Easy | Easy | Moderate | **Challenging** | Difficult

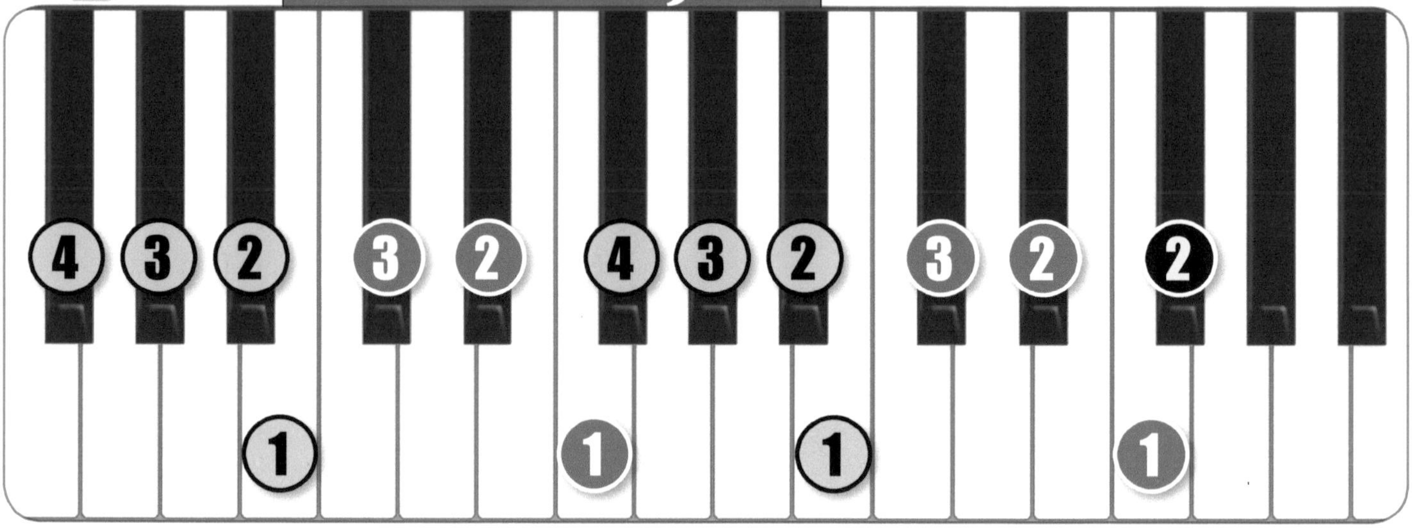

① Core Challenges

Start with these

Page		L	R	T
68	First Playthrough	☐	☐	☐
68	First from Memory	☐	☐	☐
68	First Contrary Motion	—	—	☐
68	4 Octave Tour	☐	☐	☐
69	Grand Tour	☐	☐	☐
69	Thrice is Nice	☐	☐	☐
69	10 in a Row	☐	☐	☐
69	3 Minute Quota	☐	☐	☐
70	3 Minute Tightrope	☐	☐	☐
70	Marathon Tightrope	☐	☐	☐
70	Witnessed by 6	☐	☐	☐
70	Lesson Startup	☐	☐	☐
71	Super Slow Motion	☐	☐	☐
71	Commentator	☐	☐	—
71	Splatmaster	☐	☐	—
72	By Feel Alone	☐	☐	☐
72	Tabletop Scale	☐	☐	☐
72	Repertoire	—	—	☐
72	Octave Collector	☐	☐	☐

L is Left Hand, **R** is Right Hand, **T** is Together

② Tempo Milestones

Gradually speeding it up

Metronome Setting	L	R	T	CM
♩=100 1 note per beat	☐	☐	☐	☐
♩=120 1 note per beat	☐	☐	☐	☐
♩=150 1 note per beat	☐	☐	☐	☐
♩=90 2 notes per beat	☐	☐	☐	☐
♩=105 2 notes per beat	☐	☐	☐	☐
♩=120 2 notes per beat	☐	☐	☐	☐
♩=135 2 notes per beat	☐	☐	☐	☐
♩=150 2 notes per beat	☐	☐	☐	☐
♩=80 4 notes per beat	☐	☐	☐	☐
♩=90 4 notes per beat	☐	☐	☐	☐
♩=100 4 notes per beat	☐	☐	☐	☐
♩=110 4 notes per beat	☐	☐	☐	☐
♩=120 4 notes per beat	☐	☐	☐	☐
♩=130 4 notes per beat	☐	☐	☐	☐
♩=140 4 notes per beat	☐	☐	☐	☐

CM is contrary motion. Contrary scales are 2 octaves, all others are 4 octaves. Must be **twice in a row correct**.

Very Easy | Easy | Moderate | **Challenging** | Difficult

F#/Gb Major

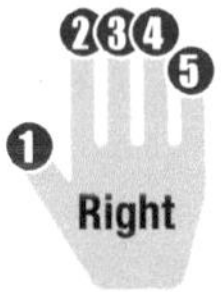

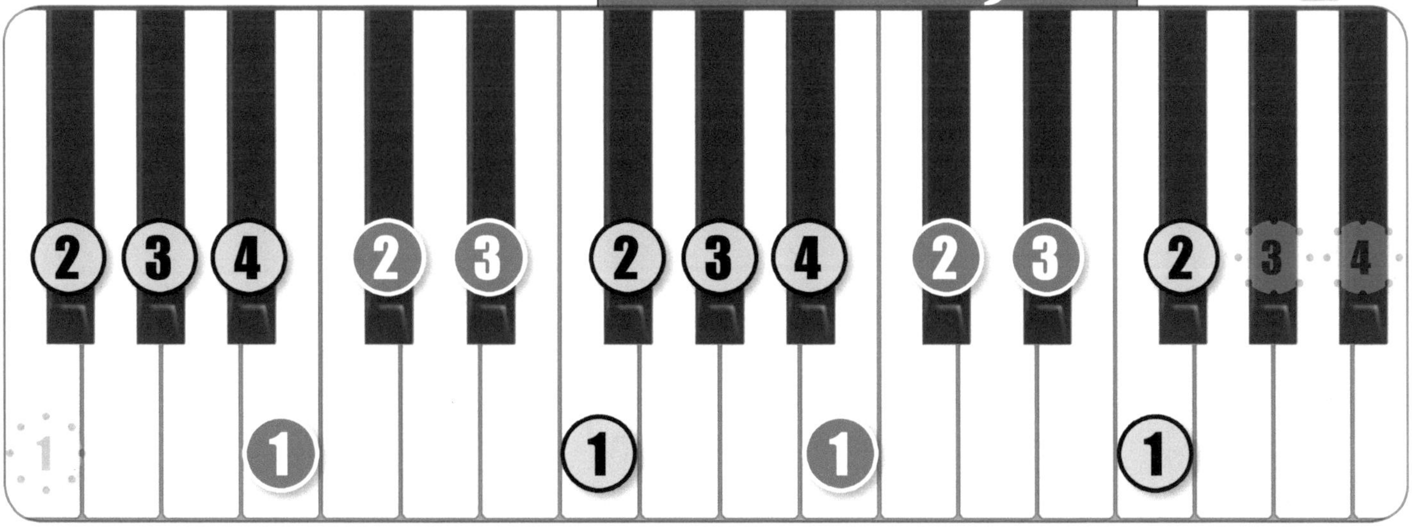

③ Twists

Brain hurtingly tough challenges

		1	2	3	4	5	6	7	8	9	10
Rhythm	**74**	☐	☐	☐	☐	☐	☐	☐	☐	☐	☐
Articulation	**76**	☐	☐	☐	☐	☐	☐	☐	☐	☐	☐
Dynamic	**78**	☐	☐	☐	☐	☐	☐	☐	☐	☐	☐
Ratio	**80**	☐	☐	☐	☐	☐	☐	☐	☐	–	–
Balance	**82**	☐	☐	☐	☐	☐	☐	☐	☐	–	–
Cacophony	**84**	☐	☐	☐	☐	☐	☐	☐	☐	☐	☐
Cascade	**86**	☐	☐	☐	☐	☐	☐	–	–	–	–
Interval	**88**	☐	☐	☐	☐	☐	☐	☐	☐	☐	☐
Contrary	**90**	☐	☐	☐	☐	☐	☐	–	–	–	–

Twists must be completed **2 hands together**

Track your Progress

Count your completed Challenges

- 1 ○ Dabbling
- 3 ○ Beginner
- **8 ○ Apprentice**
- 16 ○ Aspiring
- 27 ○ Experienced
- **41 ○ Skilled**
- 58 ○ Proficient
- 78 ○ Expert
- **101 ○ Master**
- 127 ○ Grandmaster
- 156 ○ Legendary
- **189 ○ Yours for life***

* You'll ***never*** forget this scale, even if you never practice it again.

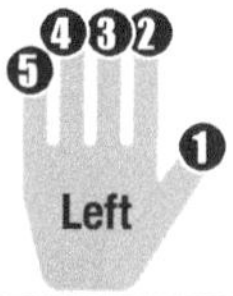

G Minor

Very Easy | **Easy** | Moderate | Challenging | Difficult

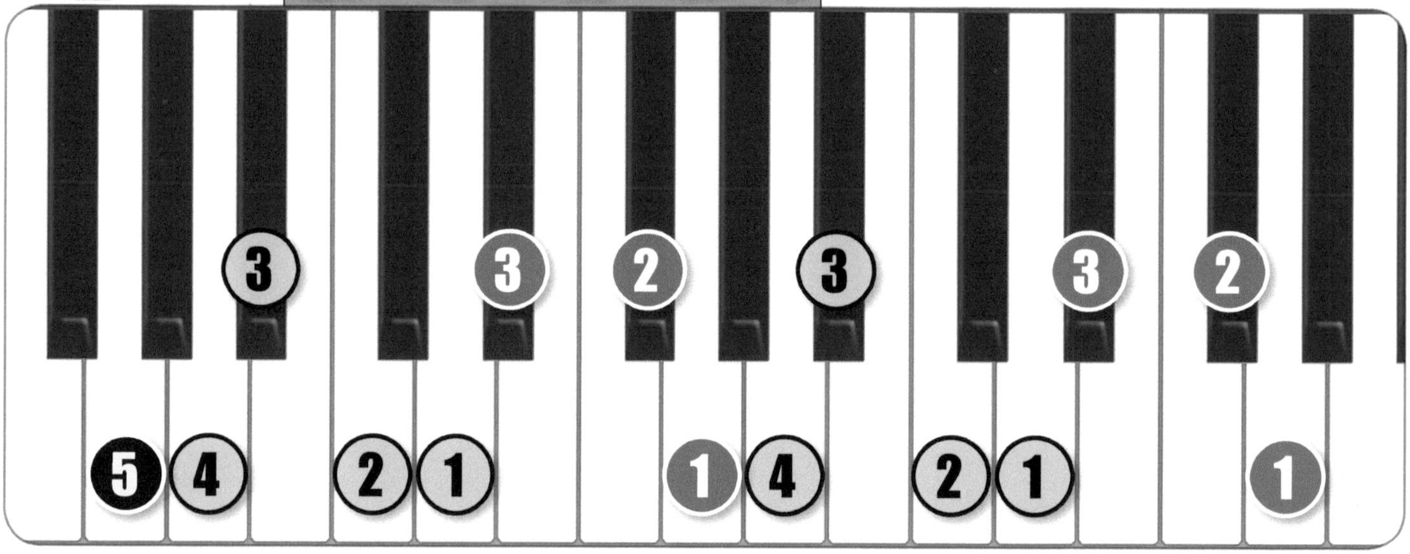

① Core Challenges

Start with these

Page		L	R	T
68	First Playthrough	☐	☐	☐
68	First from Memory	☐	☐	☐
68	First Contrary Motion	–	–	☐
68	4 Octave Tour	☐	☐	☐
69	Grand Tour	☐	☐	☐
69	Thrice is Nice	☐	☐	☐
69	10 in a Row	☐	☐	☐
69	3 Minute Quota	☐	☐	☐
70	3 Minute Tightrope	☐	☐	☐
70	Marathon Tightrope	☐	☐	☐
70	Witnessed by 6	☐	☐	☐
70	Lesson Startup	☐	☐	☐
71	Super Slow Motion	☐	☐	☐
71	Commentator	☐	☐	–
71	Splatmaster	☐	☐	–
72	By Feel Alone	☐	☐	☐
72	Tabletop Scale	☐	☐	☐
72	Repertoire	–	–	☐
72	Octave Collector	☐	☐	☐

L is Left Hand, **R** is Right Hand, **T** is Together

② Tempo Milestones

Gradually speeding it up

Metronome Setting	L	R	T	CM
♩=100 1 note per beat	☐	☐	☐	☐
♩=120 1 note per beat	☐	☐	☐	☐
♩=150 1 note per beat	☐	☐	☐	☐
♩=90 2 notes per beat	☐	☐	☐	☐
♩=105 2 notes per beat	☐	☐	☐	☐
♩=120 2 notes per beat	☐	☐	☐	☐
♩=135 2 notes per beat	☐	☐	☐	☐
♩=150 2 notes per beat	☐	☐	☐	☐
♩=80 4 notes per beat	☐	☐	☐	☐
♩=90 4 notes per beat	☐	☐	☐	☐
♩=100 4 notes per beat	☐	☐	☐	☐
♩=110 4 notes per beat	☐	☐	☐	☐
♩=120 4 notes per beat	☐	☐	☐	☐
♩=130 4 notes per beat	☐	☐	☐	☐
♩=140 4 notes per beat	☐	☐	☐	☐

CM is contrary motion. Contrary scales are 2 octaves, all others are 4 octaves. Must be **twice in a row correct**.

Very Easy | **Easy** | Moderate | Challenging | Difficult

G Minor

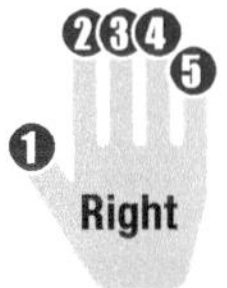

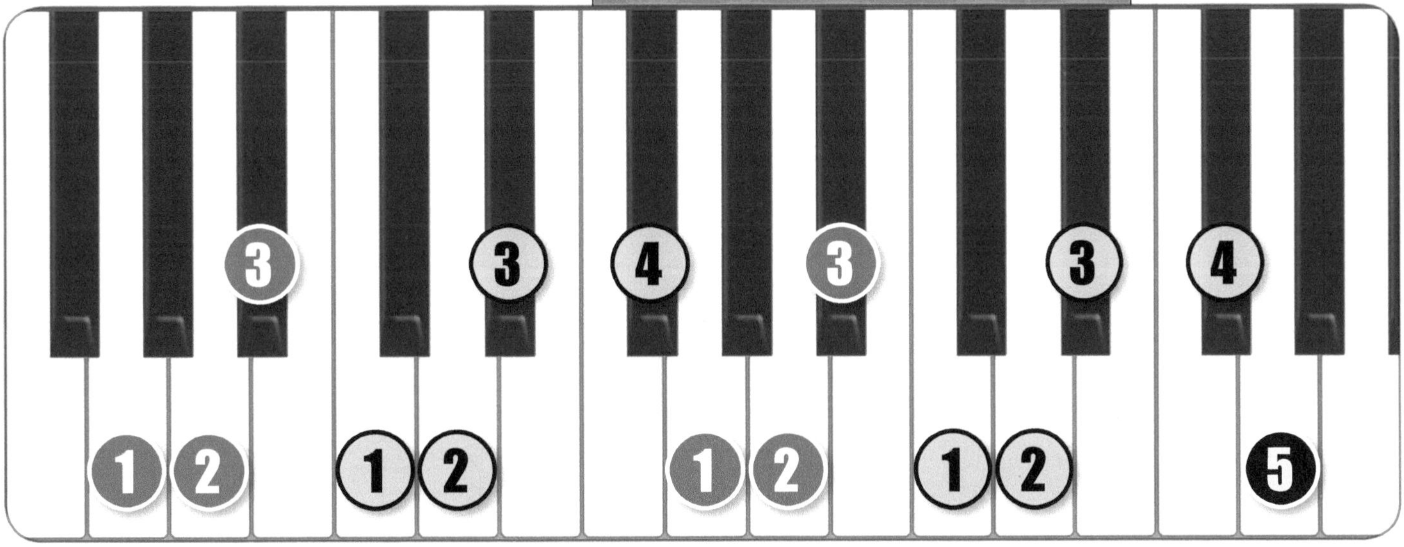

③ Twists

Brain hurtingly tough challenges

		1	2	3	4	5	6	7	8	9	10
Rhythm	**74**	☐	☐	☐	☐	☐	☐	☐	☐	☐	☐
Articulation	**76**	☐	☐	☐	☐	☐	☐	☐	☐	☐	☐
Dynamic	**78**	☐	☐	☐	☐	☐	☐	☐	☐	☐	☐
Ratio	**80**	☐	☐	☐	☐	☐	☐	☐	☐	–	–
Balance	**82**	☐	☐	☐	☐	☐	☐	☐	☐	–	–
Cacophony	**84**	☐	☐	☐	☐	☐	☐	☐	☐	☐	☐
Cascade	**86**	☐	☐	☐	☐	☐	☐	–	–	–	–
Interval	**88**	☐	☐	☐	☐	☐	☐	☐	☐	☐	☐
Contrary	**90**	☐	☐	☐	☐	☐	☐	–	–	–	–

Twists must be completed **2 hands together**

Track your Progress

Count your completed Challenges

- 1 ○ Dabbling
- 3 ○ Beginner
- **8 ○ Apprentice**
- 16 ○ Aspiring
- 27 ○ Experienced
- **41 ○ Skilled**
- 58 ○ Proficient
- 78 ○ Expert
- **101 ○ Master**
- 127 ○ Grandmaster
- 156 ○ Legendary
- **189 ○ Yours for life***

* You'll *never* forget this scale, even if you never practice it again.

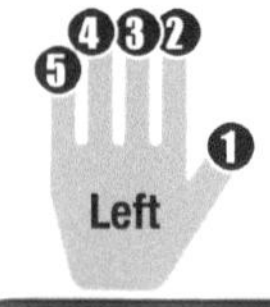

G Major

Very Easy | Easy | Moderate | Challenging | Difficult

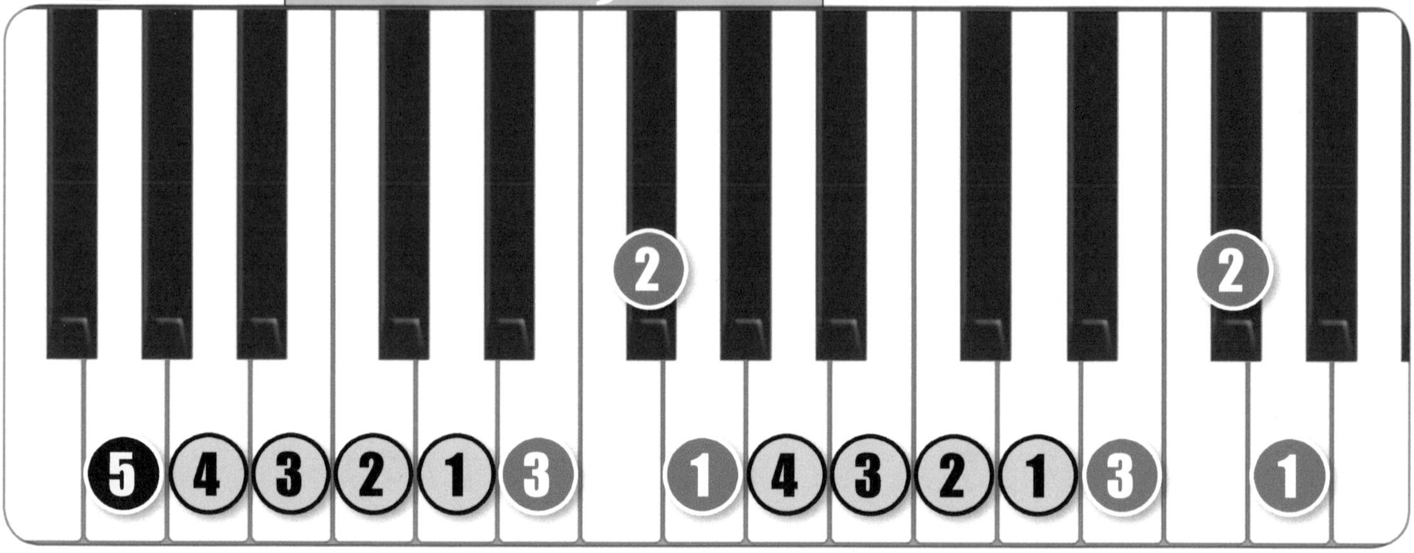

① Core Challenges

Start with these

Page		L	R	T
68	First Playthrough	☐	☐	☐
68	First from Memory	☐	☐	☐
68	First Contrary Motion	—	—	☐
68	4 Octave Tour	☐	☐	☐
69	Grand Tour	☐	☐	☐
69	Thrice is Nice	☐	☐	☐
69	10 in a Row	☐	☐	☐
69	3 Minute Quota	☐	☐	☐
70	3 Minute Tightrope	☐	☐	☐
70	Marathon Tightrope	☐	☐	☐
70	Witnessed by 6	☐	☐	☐
70	Lesson Startup	☐	☐	☐
71	Super Slow Motion	☐	☐	☐
71	Commentator	☐	☐	—
71	Splatmaster	☐	☐	—
72	By Feel Alone	☐	☐	☐
72	Tabletop Scale	☐	☐	☐
72	Repertoire	—	—	☐
72	Octave Collector	☐	☐	☐

L is Left Hand, **R** is Right Hand, **T** is Together

② Tempo Milestones

Gradually speeding it up

Metronome Setting	L	R	T	CM
♩=100 1 note per beat	☐	☐	☐	☐
♩=120 1 note per beat	☐	☐	☐	☐
♩=150 1 note per beat	☐	☐	☐	☐
♩=90 2 notes per beat	☐	☐	☐	☐
♩=105 2 notes per beat	☐	☐	☐	☐
♩=120 2 notes per beat	☐	☐	☐	☐
♩=135 2 notes per beat	☐	☐	☐	☐
♩=150 2 notes per beat	☐	☐	☐	☐
♩=80 4 notes per beat	☐	☐	☐	☐
♩=90 4 notes per beat	☐	☐	☐	☐
♩=100 4 notes per beat	☐	☐	☐	☐
♩=110 4 notes per beat	☐	☐	☐	☐
♩=120 4 notes per beat	☐	☐	☐	☐
♩=130 4 notes per beat	☐	☐	☐	☐
♩=140 4 notes per beat	☐	☐	☐	☐

CM is contrary motion. Contrary scales are 2 octaves, all others are 4 octaves. Must be **twice in a row correct**.

Very Easy | Easy | Moderate | Challenging | Difficult

G Major

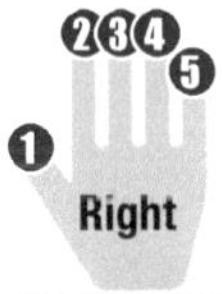

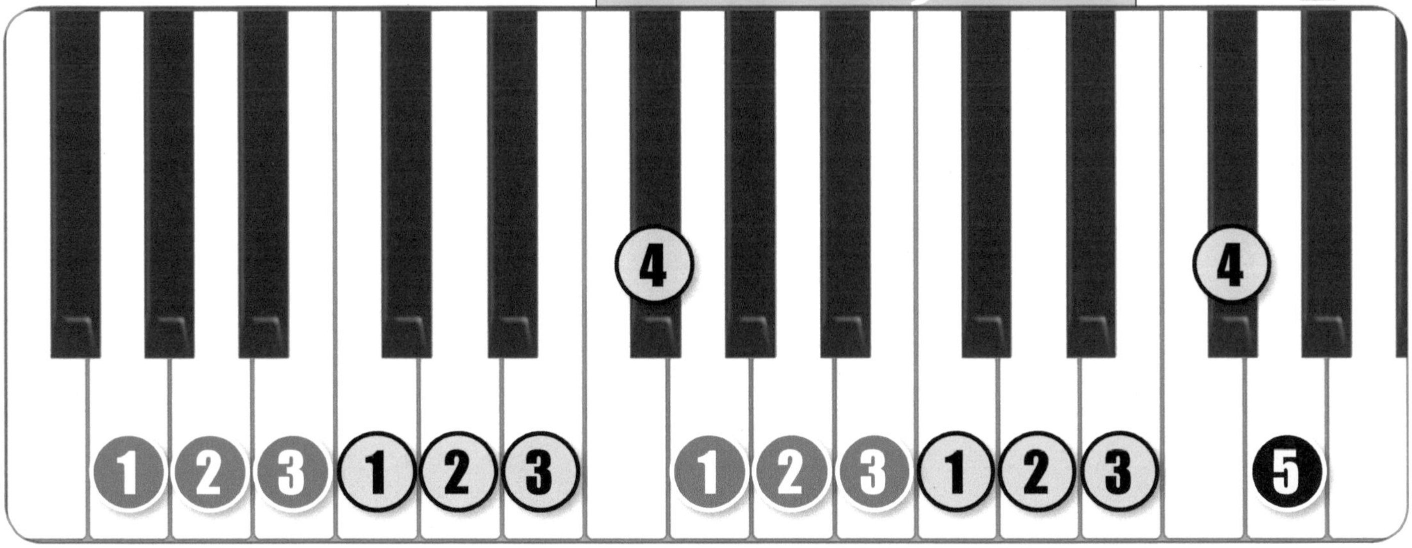

③ Twists

Brain hurtingly tough challenges

		1	2	3	4	5	6	7	8	9	10
Rhythm	**74**	☐	☐	☐	☐	☐	☐	☐	☐	☐	☐
Articulation	**76**	☐	☐	☐	☐	☐	☐	☐	☐	☐	☐
Dynamic	**78**	☐	☐	☐	☐	☐	☐	☐	☐	☐	☐
Ratio	**80**	☐	☐	☐	☐	☐	☐	☐	☐	–	–
Balance	**82**	☐	☐	☐	☐	☐	☐	☐	☐	–	–
Cacophony	**84**	☐	☐	☐	☐	☐	☐	☐	☐	☐	☐
Cascade	**86**	☐	☐	☐	☐	☐	☐	–	–	–	–
Interval	**88**	☐	☐	☐	☐	☐	☐	☐	☐	☐	☐
Contrary	**90**	☐	☐	☐	☐	☐	☐	–	–	–	–

Twists must be completed **2 hands together**

Track your Progress

Count your completed Challenges

- 1 ○ Dabbling
- 3 ○ Beginner
- **8 ○ Apprentice**
- 16 ○ Aspiring
- 27 ○ Experienced
- **41 ○ Skilled**
- 58 ○ Proficient
- 78 ○ Expert
- **101 ○ Master**
- 127 ○ Grandmaster
- 156 ○ Legendary
- **189 ○ Yours for life***

* You'll *never* forget this scale, even if you never practice it again.

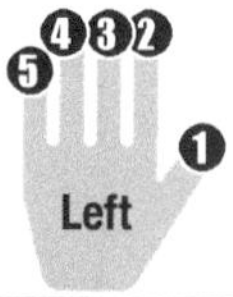

$G^{\#}$/A^{b} Minor

Very Easy | Easy | Moderate | Challenging | **Difficult**

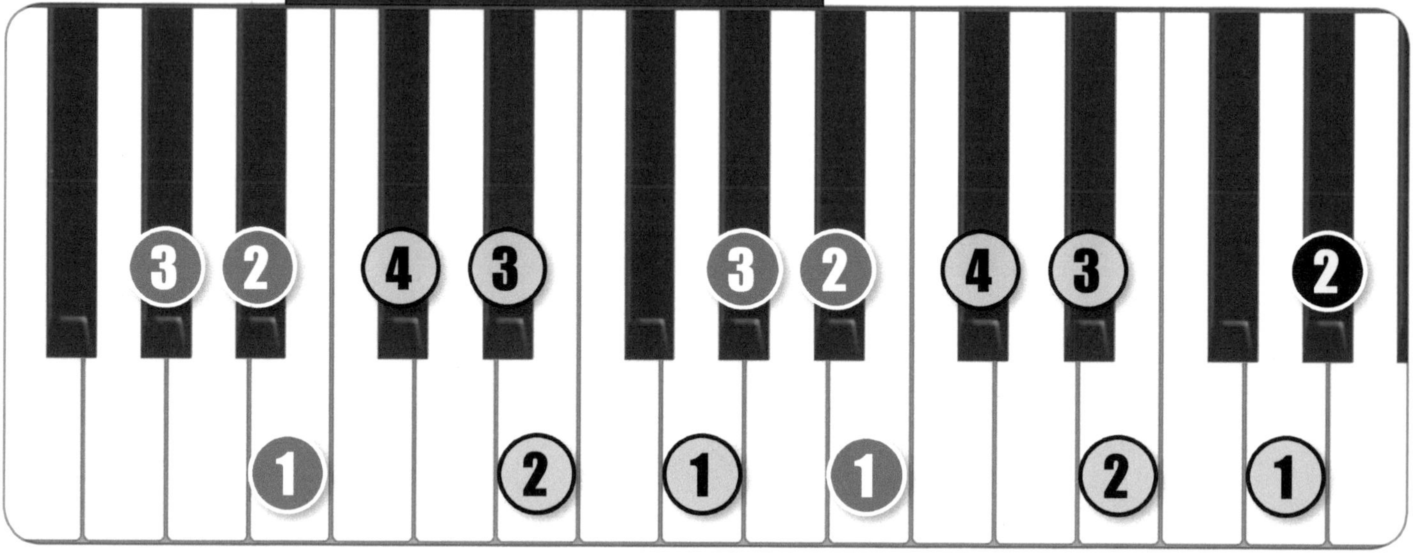

① Core Challenges

Start with these

Page		L	R	T
68	First Playthrough	☐	☐	☐
68	First from Memory	☐	☐	☐
68	First Contrary Motion	—	—	☐
68	4 Octave Tour	☐	☐	☐
69	Grand Tour	☐	☐	☐
69	Thrice is Nice	☐	☐	☐
69	10 in a Row	☐	☐	☐
69	3 Minute Quota	☐	☐	☐
70	3 Minute Tightrope	☐	☐	☐
70	Marathon Tightrope	☐	☐	☐
70	Witnessed by 6	☐	☐	☐
70	Lesson Startup	☐	☐	☐
71	Super Slow Motion	☐	☐	☐
71	Commentator	☐	☐	—
71	Splatmaster	☐	☐	—
72	By Feel Alone	☐	☐	☐
72	Tabletop Scale	☐	☐	☐
72	Repertoire	—	—	☐
72	Octave Collector	☐	☐	☐

L is Left Hand, **R** is Right Hand, **T** is Together

② Tempo Milestones

Gradually speeding it up

Metronome Setting	L	R	T	CM
♩=100 1 note per beat	☐	☐	☐	☐
♩=120 1 note per beat	☐	☐	☐	☐
♩=150 1 note per beat	☐	☐	☐	☐
♩=90 2 notes per beat	☐	☐	☐	☐
♩=105 2 notes per beat	☐	☐	☐	☐
♩=120 2 notes per beat	☐	☐	☐	☐
♩=135 2 notes per beat	☐	☐	☐	☐
♩=150 2 notes per beat	☐	☐	☐	☐
♩=80 4 notes per beat	☐	☐	☐	☐
♩=90 4 notes per beat	☐	☐	☐	☐
♩=100 4 notes per beat	☐	☐	☐	☐
♩=110 4 notes per beat	☐	☐	☐	☐
♩=120 4 notes per beat	☐	☐	☐	☐
♩=130 4 notes per beat	☐	☐	☐	☐
♩=140 4 notes per beat	☐	☐	☐	☐

CM is contrary motion. Contrary scales are 2 octaves, all others are 4 octaves. Must be **twice in a row correct**.

Very Easy | Easy | Moderate | Challenging | **Difficult**

G# / Ab Minor

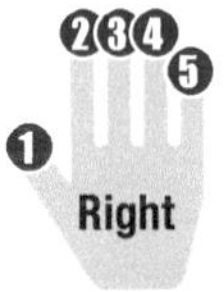

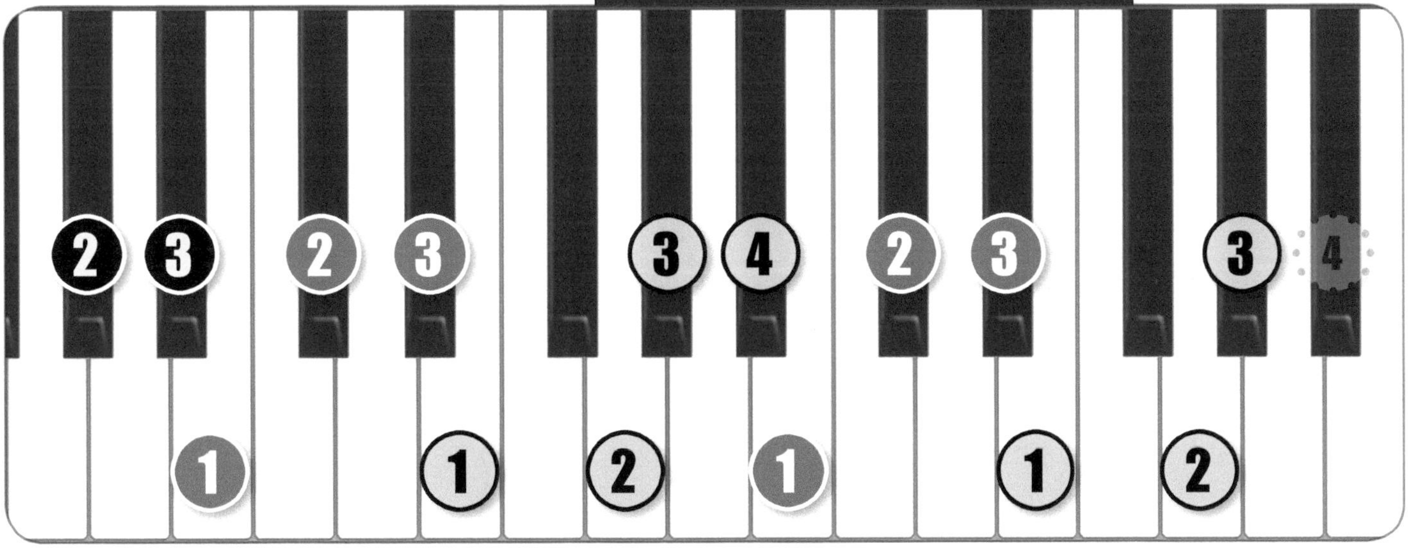

③ Twists

Brain hurtingly tough challenges

		1	2	3	4	5	6	7	8	9	10
Rhythm	**74**	☐	☐	☐	☐	☐	☐	☐	☐	☐	☐
Articulation	**76**	☐	☐	☐	☐	☐	☐	☐	☐	☐	☐
Dynamic	**78**	☐	☐	☐	☐	☐	☐	☐	☐	☐	☐
Ratio	**80**	☐	☐	☐	☐	☐	☐	☐	☐	–	–
Balance	**82**	☐	☐	☐	☐	☐	☐	☐	☐	–	–
Cacophony	**84**	☐	☐	☐	☐	☐	☐	☐	☐	☐	☐
Cascade	**86**	☐	☐	☐	☐	☐	☐	–	–	–	–
Interval	**88**	☐	☐	☐	☐	☐	☐	☐	☐	☐	☐
Contrary	**90**	☐	☐	☐	☐	☐	☐	–	–	–	–

Twists must be completed **2 hands together**

Track your Progress

Count your completed Challenges

- 1 ○ Dabbling
- 3 ○ Beginner
- **8 ○ Apprentice**
- 16 ○ Aspiring
- 27 ○ Experienced
- **41 ○ Skilled**
- 58 ○ Proficient
- 78 ○ Expert
- **101 ○ Master**
- 127 ○ Grandmaster
- 156 ○ Legendary
- **189 ○ Yours for life***

* You'll *never* forget this scale, even if you never practice it again.

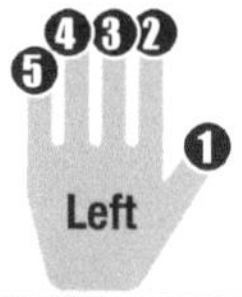

A^{b} Major

Very Easy | Easy | Moderate | **Challenging** | Difficult

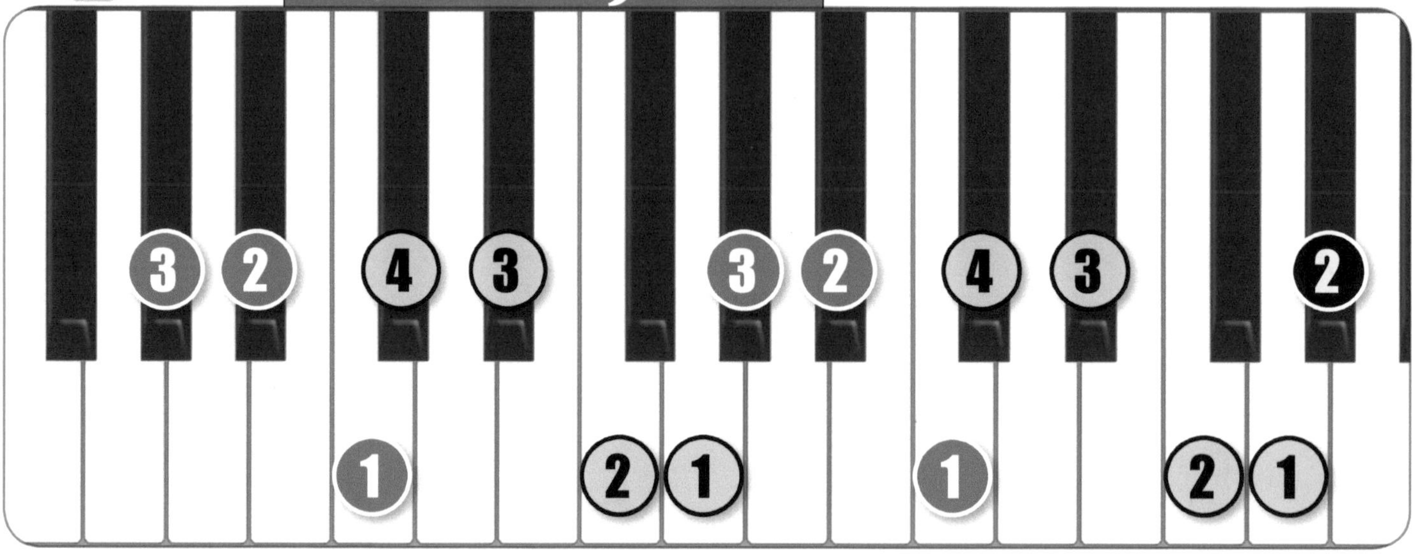

① Core Challenges

Start with these

Page		L	R	T
68	First Playthrough	☐	☐	☐
68	First from Memory	☐	☐	☐
68	First Contrary Motion	—	—	☐
68	4 Octave Tour	☐	☐	☐
69	Grand Tour	☐	☐	☐
69	Thrice is Nice	☐	☐	☐
69	10 in a Row	☐	☐	☐
69	3 Minute Quota	☐	☐	☐
70	3 Minute Tightrope	☐	☐	☐
70	Marathon Tightrope	☐	☐	☐
70	Witnessed by 6	☐	☐	☐
70	Lesson Startup	☐	☐	☐
71	Super Slow Motion	☐	☐	☐
71	Commentator	☐	☐	—
71	Splatmaster	☐	☐	—
72	By Feel Alone	☐	☐	☐
72	Tabletop Scale	☐	☐	☐
72	Repertoire	—	—	☐
72	Octave Collector	☐	☐	☐

L is Left Hand, **R** is Right Hand, **T** is Together

② Tempo Milestones

Gradually speeding it up

Metronome Setting	L	R	T	CM
♩=100 1 note per beat	☐	☐	☐	☐
♩=120 1 note per beat	☐	☐	☐	☐
♩=150 1 note per beat	☐	☐	☐	☐
♩=90 2 notes per beat	☐	☐	☐	☐
♩=105 2 notes per beat	☐	☐	☐	☐
♩=120 2 notes per beat	☐	☐	☐	☐
♩=135 2 notes per beat	☐	☐	☐	☐
♩=150 2 notes per beat	☐	☐	☐	☐
♩=80 4 notes per beat	☐	☐	☐	☐
♩=90 4 notes per beat	☐	☐	☐	☐
♩=100 4 notes per beat	☐	☐	☐	☐
♩=110 4 notes per beat	☐	☐	☐	☐
♩=120 4 notes per beat	☐	☐	☐	☐
♩=130 4 notes per beat	☐	☐	☐	☐
♩=140 4 notes per beat	☐	☐	☐	☐

CM is contrary motion. Contrary scales are 2 octaves, all others are 4 octaves. Must be **twice in a row correct**.

Very Easy | Easy | Moderate | **Challenging** | Difficult

A^{b} Major

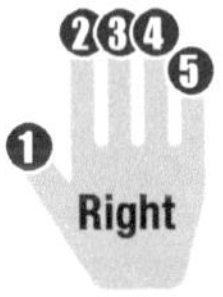

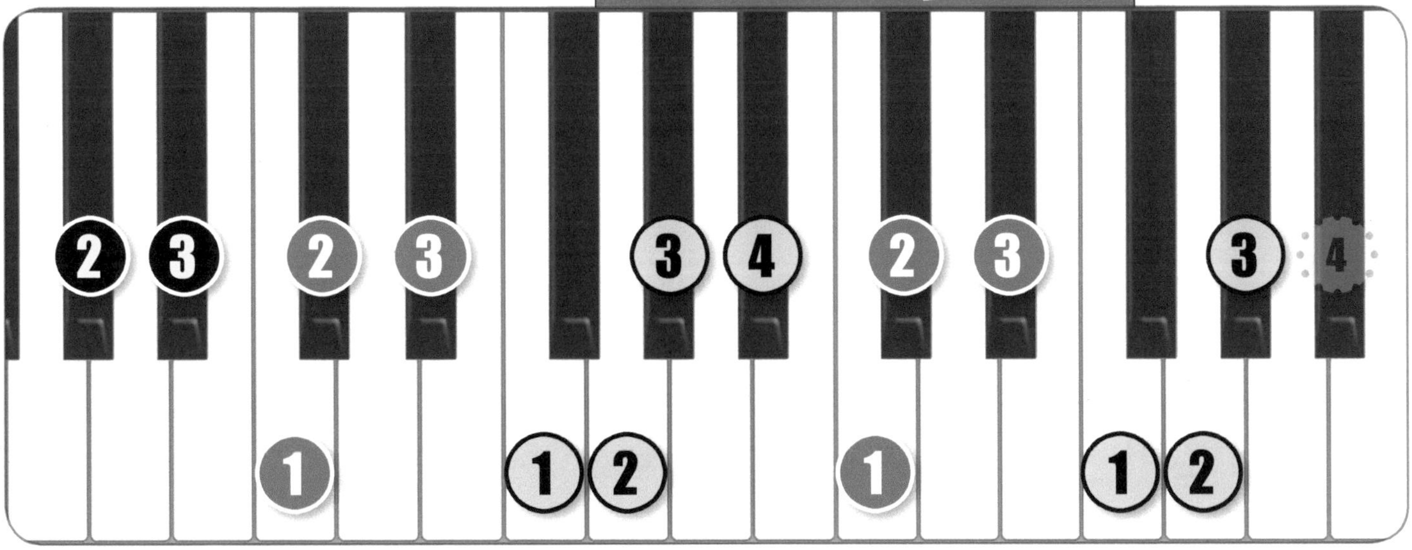

③ Twists

Brain hurtingly tough challenges

		1	2	3	4	5	6	7	8	9	10
Rhythm	**74**	☐	☐	☐	☐	☐	☐	☐	☐	☐	☐
Articulation	**76**	☐	☐	☐	☐	☐	☐	☐	☐	☐	☐
Dynamic	**78**	☐	☐	☐	☐	☐	☐	☐	☐	☐	☐
Ratio	**80**	☐	☐	☐	☐	☐	☐	☐	☐	–	–
Balance	**82**	☐	☐	☐	☐	☐	☐	☐	☐	–	–
Cacophony	**84**	☐	☐	☐	☐	☐	☐	☐	☐	☐	☐
Cascade	**86**	☐	☐	☐	☐	☐	☐	–	–	–	–
Interval	**88**	☐	☐	☐	☐	☐	☐	☐	☐	☐	☐
Contrary	**90**	☐	☐	☐	☐	☐	☐	–	–	–	–

Twists must be completed **2 hands together**

Track your Progress

Count your completed Challenges

- 1 ○ Dabbling
- 3 ○ Beginner
- **8 ○ Apprentice**
- 16 ○ Aspiring
- 27 ○ Experienced
- **41 ○ Skilled**
- 58 ○ Proficient
- 78 ○ Expert
- **101 ○ Master**
- 127 ○ Grandmaster
- 156 ○ Legendary
- **189 ○ Yours for life***

* You'll *never* forget this scale, even if you never practice it again.

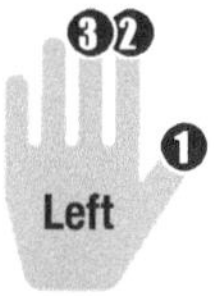

Chromatic

Very Easy | **Easy** | Moderate | Challenging | Difficult

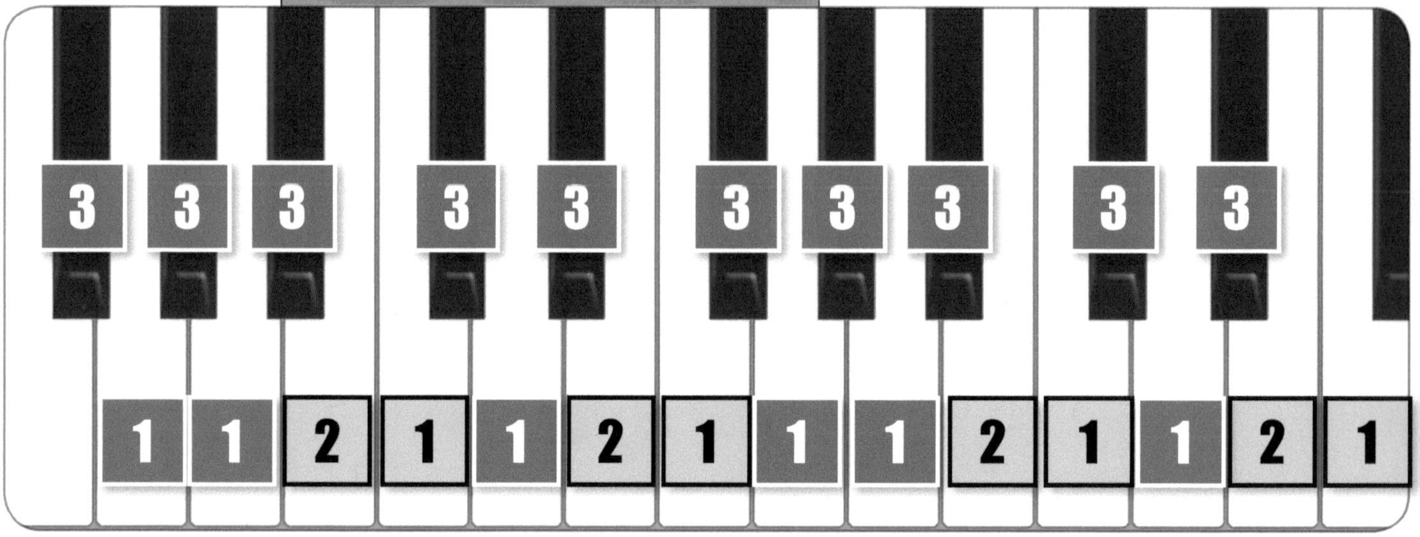

① Core Challenges

Start with these

Fingerings above are correct no matter which note your chromatic scale starts on

		C	C#	D	Eb	E	F	F#	G	Ab	A	Bb	B
68	First Playthrough **(LH)**	☐	☐	☐	☐	☐	☐	☐	☐	☐	☐	☐	☐
	First Playthrough **(RH)**	☐	☐	☐	☐	☐	☐	☐	☐	☐	☐	☐	☐
	First Playthrough **(TOG)**	☐	☐	☐	☐	☐	☐	☐	☐	☐	☐	☐	☐
68	First from Memory **(LH)**	☐	☐	☐	☐	☐	☐	☐	☐	☐	☐	☐	☐
	First from Memory **(RH)**	☐	☐	☐	☐	☐	☐	☐	☐	☐	☐	☐	☐
	First from Memory **(TOG)**	☐	☐	☐	☐	☐	☐	☐	☐	☐	☐	☐	☐
68	4 Octave Tour **(LH)**	☐	☐	☐	☐	☐	☐	☐	☐	☐	☐	☐	☐
	4 Octave Tour **(RH)**	☐	☐	☐	☐	☐	☐	☐	☐	☐	☐	☐	☐
	4 Octave Tour **(TOG)**	☐	☐	☐	☐	☐	☐	☐	☐	☐	☐	☐	☐
69	Grand Tour **(LH)**	☐	☐	☐	☐	☐	☐	☐	☐	☐	☐	☐	☐
	Grand Tour **(RH)**	☐	☐	☐	☐	☐	☐	☐	☐	☐	☐	☐	☐
	Grand Tour **(TOG)**	☐	☐	☐	☐	☐	☐	☐	☐	☐	☐	☐	☐
70	3 Minute Tightrope **(LH)**	☐	☐	☐	☐	☐	☐	☐	☐	☐	☐	☐	☐
	3 Minute Tightrope **(RH)**	☐	☐	☐	☐	☐	☐	☐	☐	☐	☐	☐	☐
	3 Minute Tightrope **(TOG)**	☐	☐	☐	☐	☐	☐	☐	☐	☐	☐	☐	☐
69	Ten in a Row **(LH)**	☐	☐	☐	☐	☐	☐	☐	☐	☐	☐	☐	☐
	Ten in a Row **(RH)**	☐	☐	☐	☐	☐	☐	☐	☐	☐	☐	☐	☐
	Ten in a Row **(TOG)**	☐	☐	☐	☐	☐	☐	☐	☐	☐	☐	☐	☐
71	Super Slow Motion **(LH)**	☐	☐	☐	☐	☐	☐	☐	☐	☐	☐	☐	☐
	Super Slow Motion **(RH)**	☐	☐	☐	☐	☐	☐	☐	☐	☐	☐	☐	☐
	Super Slow Motion **(TOG)**	☐	☐	☐	☐	☐	☐	☐	☐	☐	☐	☐	☐
68	First Contrary Motion **(TOG)**	☐	☐	☐	☐	☐	☐	☐	☐	☐	☐	☐	☐

Starting note for each Achievement is shown across the top. So the Achievement shown top left will have your LH starting on a C, turning around on the C two octaves above, and then coming back to where you started. The next tick along would be C# to C#, and so on.

Very Easy | **Easy** | Moderate | Challenging | Difficult

Chromatic

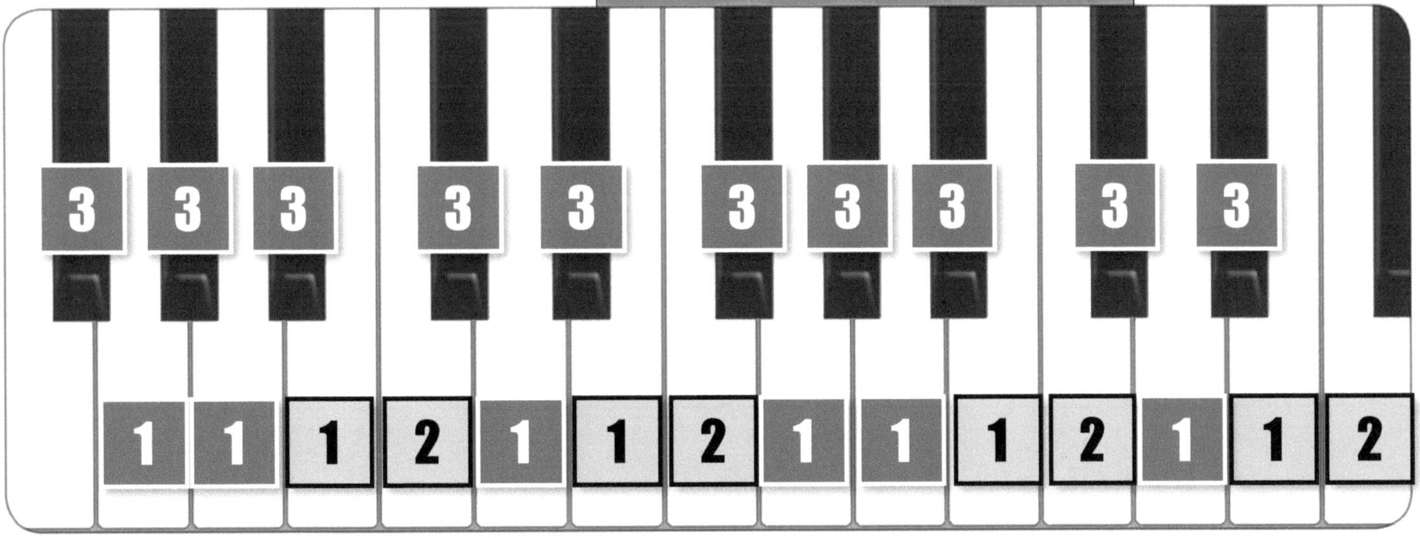

② Tempo Milestones

Gradually speeding it up

	L	R	T	CM
: ♩=100, 1 note per beat	☐	☐	☐	☐
#: ♩=120, 1 note per beat	☐	☐	☐	☐
: ♩=150, 1 note per beat	☐	☐	☐	☐
b: ♩=90, 2 notes per beat	☐	☐	☐	☐
: ♩=105, 2 notes per beat	☐	☐	☐	☐
: ♩=120, 2 notes per beat	☐	☐	☐	☐
#: ♩=135, 2 notes per beat	☐	☐	☐	☐
: ♩=150, 2 notes per beat	☐	☐	☐	☐
b: ♩=80, 4 notes per beat	☐	☐	☐	☐
: ♩=90, 4 notes per beat	☐	☐	☐	☐
b: ♩=100, 4 notes per beat	☐	☐	☐	☐
: ♩=110, 4 notes per beat	☐	☐	☐	☐
: ♩=120, 4 notes per beat	☐	☐	☐	☐
#: ♩=130, 4 notes per beat	☐	☐	☐	☐
: ♩=140, 4 notes per beat	☐	☐	☐	☐

M" is contrary motion. Contrary scales are 2 octaves, all others are octaves. Must be **twice in a row correct** to earn the Achievement.

Track your Progress

Count your completed Challenges

- 1 ○ Dabbling
- 5 ○ Beginner
- **16 ○ Apprentice**
- 32 ○ Aspiring
- 50 ○ Experienced
- **75 ○ Skilled**
- 105 ○ Proficient
- 140 ○ Expert
- **180 ○ Master**
- 222 ○ Grandmaster
- 270 ○ Legendary
- **324 ○ Yours for life***

* You'll *never* forget this scale, even if you never practice it again.

How to finger Chromatics

Chromatic scales use all 12 notes in each octave, so the 1-2-3, 1-2-3-4 pattern that works so well for the 7 notes of Major and Minor scales won't work here.

Fortunately the fingering that does work is easy to figure out.

If keyboards endlessly alternated black and white notes, no matter which hand you used, chromatic fingering would look like this:

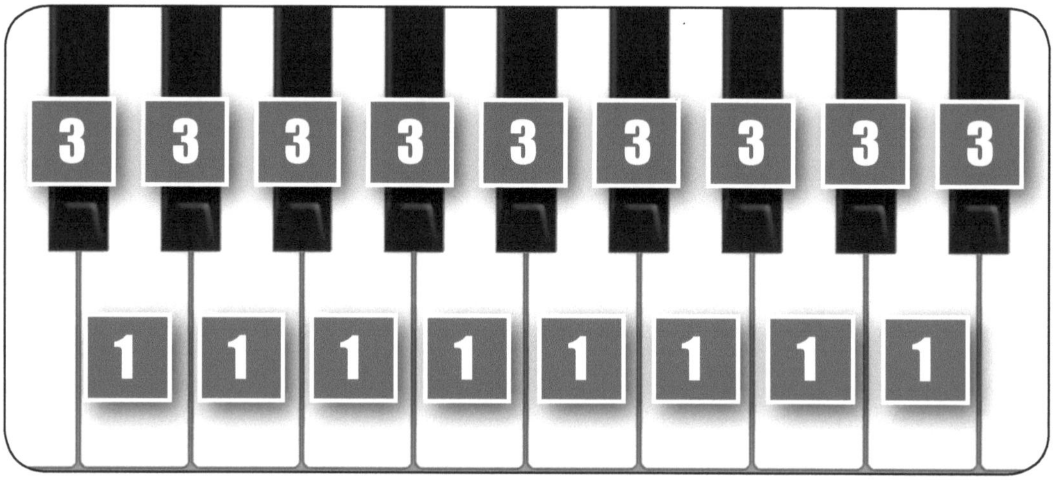

It's a strong fingering; the long 3rd finger works well on black notes, while the (much shorter) thumb takes care of white notes. Easy to play, easy to remember.

The good news is that real keyboards almost—almost—allow this endless 3-1-3-1 sequence. What messes it up is that every so often there are two white notes in a row:

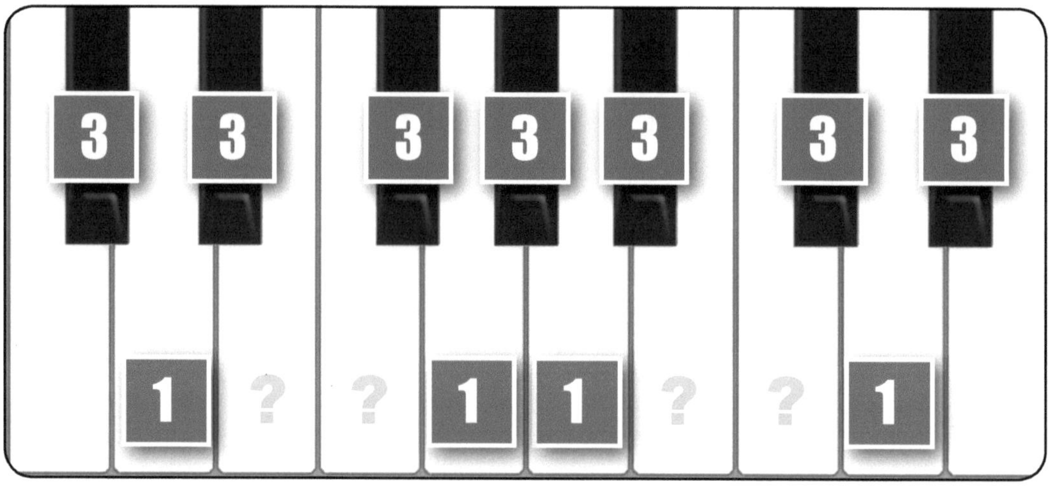

You can see that you'll still use 3-1-3-1 whenever the black and white notes alternate, which is most of each octave. But how do you finger the consecutive white notes?

The solution is that you still get to use your **thumb** on one note in each pair, and make up the extra with your **2nd finger** on the other.

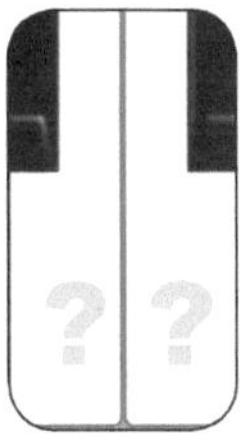

But which way around though? 1-2 or 2-1?

The answer to this question is the only tricky thing about chromatic scales: *it depends which hand you're using.* To figure it out, just **look at the back of your hands** and notice the order in which 1 and 2 naturally fall:

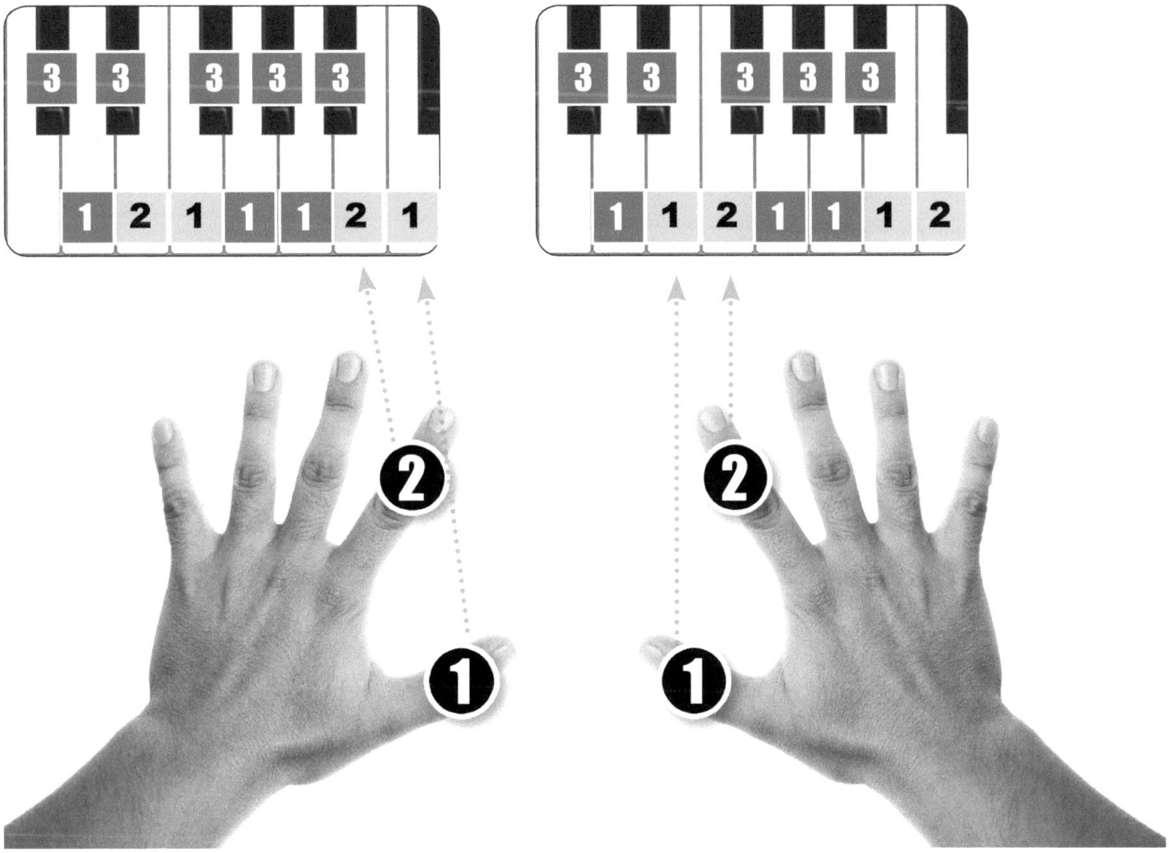

A quick glance like this will confirm that your **left hand** will always use 2 on the lower of the two white notes, 1 on the higher. Your **right hand** will be the other way around.

But otherwise, you're still spending most of your time happily playing 3-1-3-1. As long as you're careful whenever there are consecutive white notes, chromatics really are very easy.

Core Challenges

Bootcamp's quests, explained

Core Challenges

Bootcamp's quests, explained

Assume **zero errors** to complete each Challenge, unless told otherwise.

Turn to **Page 13** to find your scales.

☑ First Playthrough

To complete this Challenge...
Play the scale **once.**

Scale settings
Octaves: 2

Speed: Up to you

Memory: Up to you

Notes
Couldn't be easier. Play the scale just *once*—at any speed you like—with or without this book in front of you, and you've completed the Challenge. Of course, not all your Challenges will be this friendly...

☑ First from Memory

To complete this Challenge...
Play the scale once **from memory.**

Scale settings
Octaves: 2

Speed: Up to you

Memory: Yes

Notes
Exactly the same as the "First Playthrough" challenge, but this time there's no reference in front of you.

☑ First Contrary Motion

To complete this Challenge...
Play the scale once **contrary motion.**

Scale settings
Octaves: 2 in each hand

Speed: Up to you

Memory: Up to you

Notes
You know how this works—both hands start on the same note, right hand plays up, left hand plays down. Turn around after two octaves, and the hands play back towards each other again. Once you've done this, you might want to start work on the Contrary Twists (p90)

☑ 4 Octave Tour

To complete this Challenge...
Play a **four octave version** of this scale.

Scale settings
Octaves: 4

Speed: Up to you

Memory: Yes

Notes
4 octave scales might actually be easier than 2 octave scales. Why? Because **bookends** and **ghosts** (see p 7-9) *only happen at the top and bottom of scales*. It's nothing but regular 1-2-3 and 1-2-3-4 in the middle... so the longer the middle, the easier the ride. Note that this Challenge is also "from memory".

Core Challenges

Bootcamp's quests, explained

Assume **zero errors** to complete each Challenge, unless told otherwise.

Turn to **Page 13** to find your scales.

☑ Grand Tour

To complete this Challenge...

Play the version of this scale that **covers the entire keyboard**.

Scale settings

Octaves: As many as you can fit on your keyboard

Speed: Up to you

Memory: Yes

Notes

If you were playing D Major, you'd start on the lowest D on the piano, play up until you get to the highest D, then turn around and play back down again. The number of octaves will vary depending on the key of the scale and how many notes your keyboard has.

☑ Thrice is nice

To complete this Challenge...

Play the scale **three times in a row** without error.

Scale settings

Octaves: 2

Speed: Up to you

Memory: Yes

Notes

It's the "in a row" that makes this tricky—a tiny mistake on the very last note of the third playthrough will actually send you right back to the beginning of the *first* playthrough. The first of a series of your-scales-under-pressure Challenges.

☑ 10 in a Row

To complete this Challenge...

Play the scale **ten times in a row** without error.

Scale settings

Octaves: 2

Speed: Up to you

Memory: Yes

Notes

As for Thrice is nice, it's the "in a row" that's the killer. A tough test—again, just one slip will send you back to the start of the *first* playthrough.

☑ 3 Minute Quota

To complete this Challenge...

Play the scale **25 times** correctly within a **3 minute time limit**.

Scale settings

Octaves: 2

Speed: Up to you

Memory: Yes

Notes

A mistake won't reset the count, but will eat time, because only clean playthroughs count towards your total. To fit 25 clean playthroughs in, you can't afford to play too slowly...but you also can't afford to lose time with mistakes. A tough balancing act when you're choosing your tempo.

Core Challenges

Bootcamp's quests, explained

Assume **zero errors** to complete each Challenge, unless told otherwise.

Turn to **Page 13** to find your scales.

☑ 3 Minute Tightrope

To complete this Challenge...

Play the scale for **three minutes continuously** without a single mistake.

Scale settings

Octaves: 2

Speed: Played as ♪, at least ♩=120

Memory: Yes

Notes

Make sure there's a metronome running to enforce the minimum speed requirement. This is a demanding test...just one slip, and the time starts again. Three minutes has never felt so long...

☑ Marathon Tightrope

To complete this Challenge...

Play the scale **fifty times(!) in a row** without error.

Scale settings

Octaves: 2

Speed: Up to you

Memory: Yes

Notes

Many have tried. Few have succeeded. This Challenge is the emperor of all the pressure achievements—and the more successful playthroughs, the more intense the pressure becomes. Your 50th lap will be a supreme test of your nerves and focus, because you'll know that one slip…just one…and you go right back to the start…

☑ Witnessed by 6

To complete this Challenge...

Play the scale in front of a total of **six different people**.

Scale settings

Octaves: 2

Speed: Up to you

Memory: Yes

Notes

It doesn't have to be six people all at once—if you play the scale for your **parents** in the morning, a **friend** in the afternoon, and your **little sister** the next day, that's four people already. Only two to go. (Your teacher counts as a person too, by the way)

☑ Lesson Startup

To complete this Challenge...

To have **started a lesson** with this scale, no mistakes, **first attempt**.

Scale settings

Octaves: 2

Speed: Up to you

Memory: Up to your teacher

Notes

This is a sudden death Challenge that you can only attempt once in each lesson. No warmups. Get through it without a mistake and the tick is yours—otherwise, you have to wait until the next lesson to try again.

Core Challenges

Bootcamp's quests, explained

Assume **zero errors** to complete each Challenge, unless told otherwise.

Turn to **Page 13** to find your scales.

☑ Super Slow Motion

To complete this Challenge...

Play the scale once through with no mistakes at **60bpm**, **4 beats per note**.

Scale settings

Octaves: 4(!)

Speed: Played as 𝅝; ♩=60

Memory: Yes

Notes

You heard right—it's 4 beats *per note* (not 4 notes per beat). Normally playing more slowly makes things easier, but when the tempo get this slow, your mind can start to play tricks...you'll have 4 seconds between each note(!) to doubt, to wonder, to question...

☑ Commentator

To complete this Challenge...

To ***describe*** the notes & fingering of the entire scale, **without actually playing anything.**

Scale settings

Octaves: 2—describe up and back

Speed: N/A

Memory: Yes

Notes

So for the left hand of A Major, you'd sound something like this: "*I'd start with my 5th finger playing an A, then move to my 4th finger on the B. My 3rd finger would be next on the C#, followed by my 2nd on the D, and the thumb on the E...*"

☑ Splatmaster

To complete this Challenge...

Play the scale once through in **"splats"** (see below)

Scale settings

Octaves: As many as you can fit on your keyboard

Speed: Up to you

Memory: Up to you

Notes

Instead of playing the notes one after the other, you'll be playing *all notes in the same fingering group simultaneously*—a "splat".

So a fingering group of 1-2-3 would be one splat—a cluster featuring all three notes at the same time. The group of 1-2-3-4 that follows would then be played as another splat. Bookends and incompletes are treated as separate splats.

An example: the Left Hand of G Major ascending (see p 58) would be played as

1. Solitary G (5th finger, bookend)
2. SPLAT cluster of ABCD (4-3-2-1 group)
3. SPLAT cluster of E-F#-G (3-2-1 group)
4. SPLAT cluster of ABCD (4-3-2-1 group)
5. SPLAT cluster of E-F#-G (3-2-1 group)

Descend by following the steps in reverse.

In this way, you can compresss a 29 note 2 octave scale into just 8 splats + 2 bookends—a powerful way to reinforce exactly where the fingering groups are, and a tidy way to practice scales when time is short.

Core Challenges

Bootcamp's quests, explained

Assume **zero errors** to complete each Challenge, unless told otherwise.

Turn to **Page 13** to find your scales.

☑ By Feel Alone

To complete this Challenge...

Play the scale once through **with your eyes closed.**

Scale settings

Octaves: 4

Speed: Up to you

Memory: Yes (obviously)

Notes

This Challenge is surprisingly easy if you know the scale well. But if there is anything you're not sure about—*anything*—the scale will disappear into the fog. Even just *attempting* this Challenge is a great way to pinpoint exactly where in the scale any uncertainty might be.

☑ Tabletop Scale

To complete this Challenge...

Play the scale once through **on a tabletop**.

Scale settings

Octaves: 2

Speed: Up to you

Memory: Yes

Notes

There's no keyboard in sight, but you'll still need to be placing your fingers where the notes *would* have been. Anybody watching you should clearly be able to tell whether each finger stroke would have been on a black or white note—your picture of the scale will have to be very clear to complete this Challenge.

☑ Repertoire

To complete this Challenge...

To have **performed a piece** in the key of this scale.

Scale settings

Octaves: N/A

Speed: N/A

Memory: Up to you

Notes

The piece doesn't necessarily need to feature scale passages, just to be in the same key as the scale you're trying to earn this tick for. This Challenge is one of the most powerful in the collection—there is no better way to test a scale than to have actually performed a piece that is *built* from those very notes.

☑ Octave Collector

To complete this Challenge...

Collect 250 octaves of this scale

Scale settings

Octaves: Varies

Speed: Up to you

Memory: Up to you

Notes

You "collect" octaves every time you complete an error-free playthrough of a scale, and your total is cumulative. So...if you were working on the right hand of Bb minor, and you played a 2 octave version of the scale 5 times before completing a Grand Tour (see p69) of 7 octaves, you would have already collected (2x5)+7=17 octaves. Only 233 octaves to go...

Twists

Extra tough challenges to prove your mastery

Probably the most famous scale rhythm of them all

Rhythm Twist 1

Triplets with stopovers on the keynote

Rhythm Twist 2

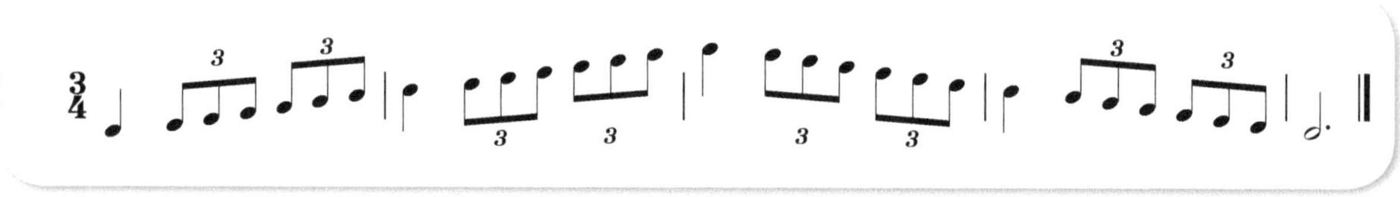

Has you playing pairs of notes fast— forcing half the fingering transitions to be quick . . .

Rhythm Twist 3

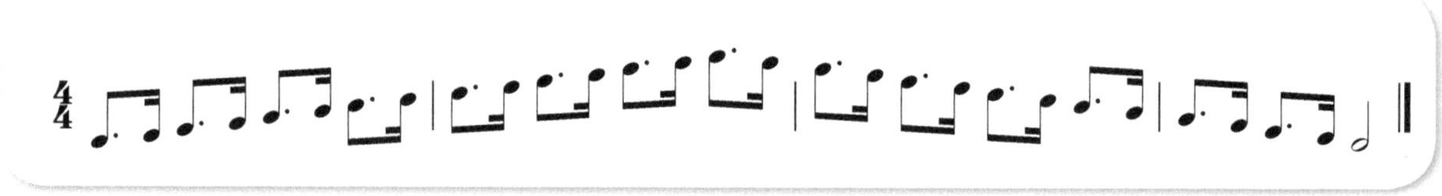

...and now reversed, to target the remaining transitions

Rhythm Twist 4

Start of each octave tumbles out quickly, then the speed halves each beat thereafter

Rhythm Twist 5

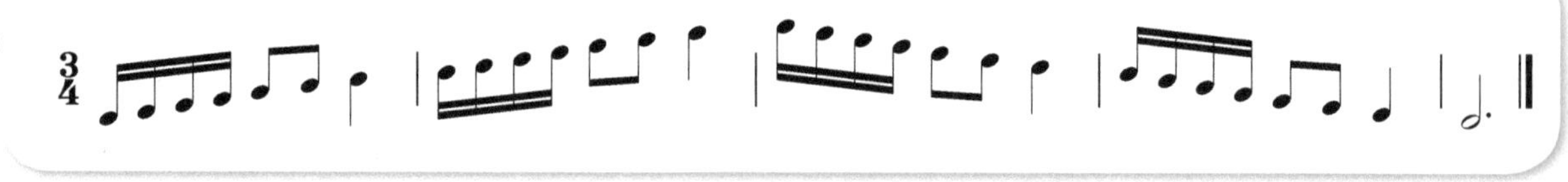

Twists: Rhythm

Rhythm Twist 6

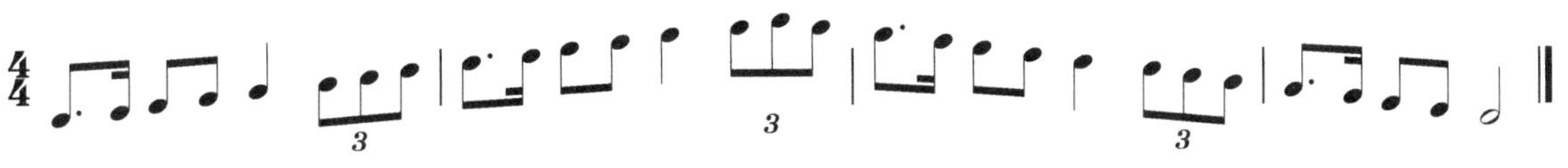

Notice how the different rhythms force different finger transitions to be rapid or delayed

Rhythm Twist 7

This rhythm repeats, but after two octaves, rather than one

Rhythm Twist 8

Be careful what tempo you choose for the first measure, or the second measure will be unplayable

Rhythm Twist 9

How well do you really know the scale? It will need to be on autopilot while you supervise this chaotic rhythm

Rhythm Twist 10

All staccato,
except for the keynote

Articulation Twist 1

Alternating notes staccato,
awkwardly short 2 note phrases

Articulation Twist 2

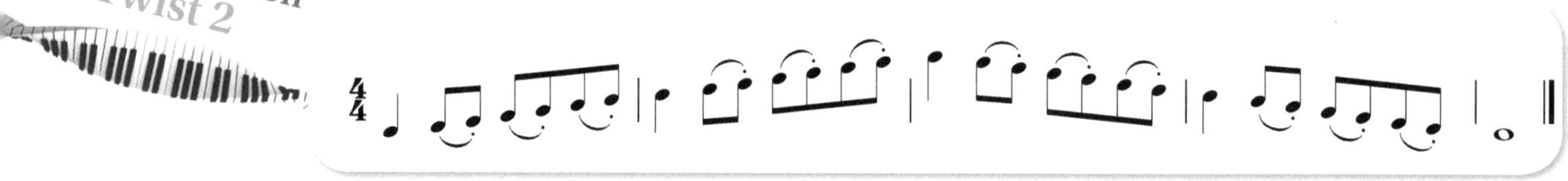

Each phrase takes you through to the next
keynote, no staccatos this time

Articulation Twist 3

Long, luxurious 2 octave legato lines

Articulation Twist 4

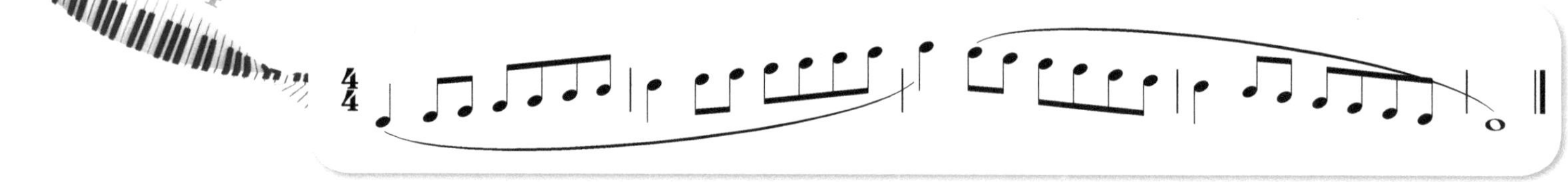

Heavy accents on 2nd, 3rd
and 4th beats

Articulation Twist 5

Twists: Articulation

As for Twist 5, but with accents shifted to the offbeats

Articulation Twist 6

Starting each octave staccato, ending legato

Articulation Twist 7

Really starting to mix it up now, pattern doesn't repeat until you're coming down

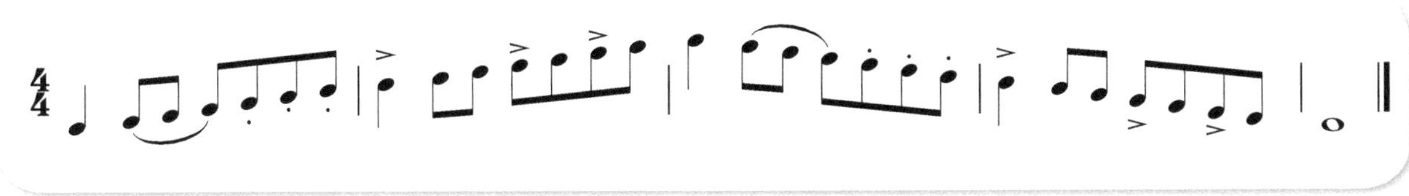

Articulation Twist 8

More crazy mixed up articulations—very easy to mess up the scale itself while your focus is on the markings (that's the point)

Articulation Twist 9

Don't bother to look for patterns. There aren't any. Impossible unless you know the scale very well

Articulation Twist 10

Just how quietly can you play? Make sure the thumb transitions are pianissimo too

Dynamic Twist 1

Notice how the forte scale makes different physical demands of you

Dynamic Twist 2

Can you actually make each note louder than the note before it...without arriving at ff too early?

Dynamic Twist 3

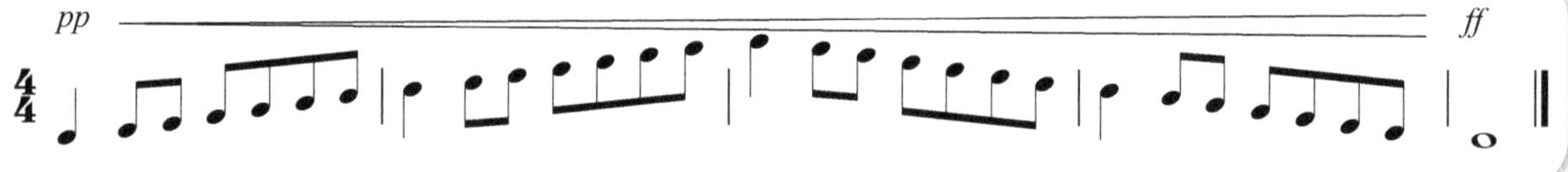

Same gradual ramp as Twist 3, but in reverse

Dynamic Twist 4

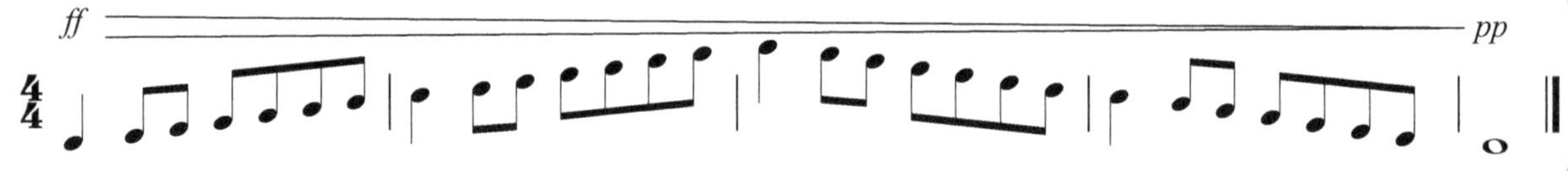

Classic arch-shaped phrase over the four bars.

Dynamic Twist 5

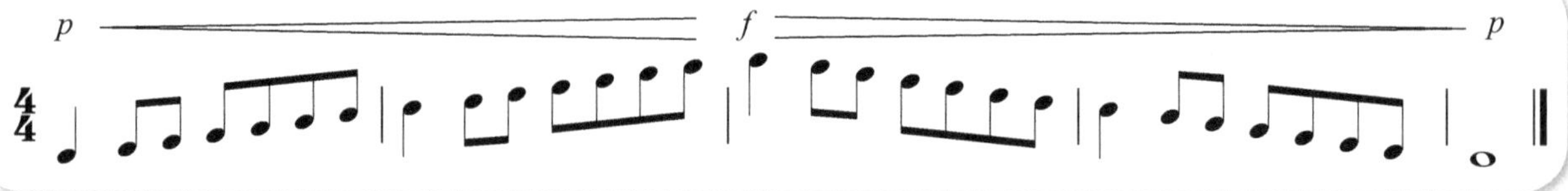

Twists: Dynamic

Dynamic Twist 6

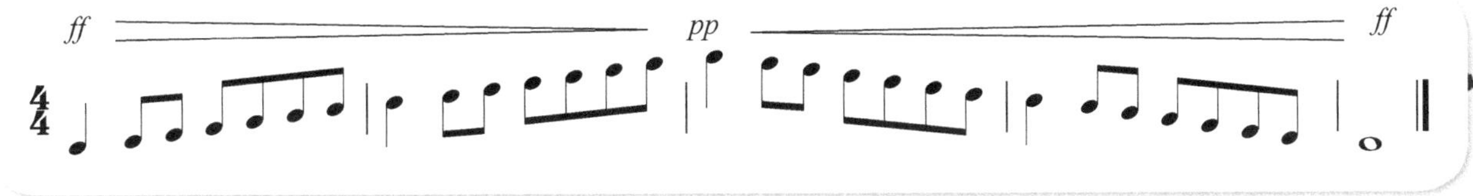

Twist 5 in reverse, and with more extreme dynamic range

Dynamic Twist 7

Mirror images...and plenty of changes to supervise, leaving you less brainpower for the scale itself

Dynamic Twist 8

"Terraced Dynamics" means that the changes are sudden... no crescendos or diminuendos to smooth things out

Dynamic Twist 9

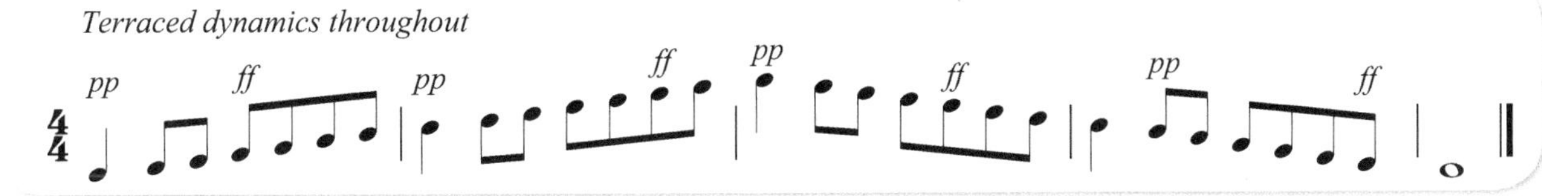

The kitchen sink...and a final note that would make no sound at all if it were any quieter

Dynamic Twist 10

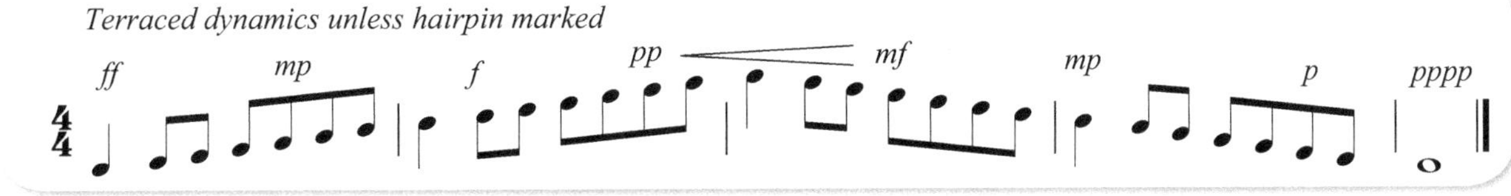

Right hand plays one octave, while...

Ratio Twist 1

...Left hand plays two octaves, twice as fast

Ratio Twist 2

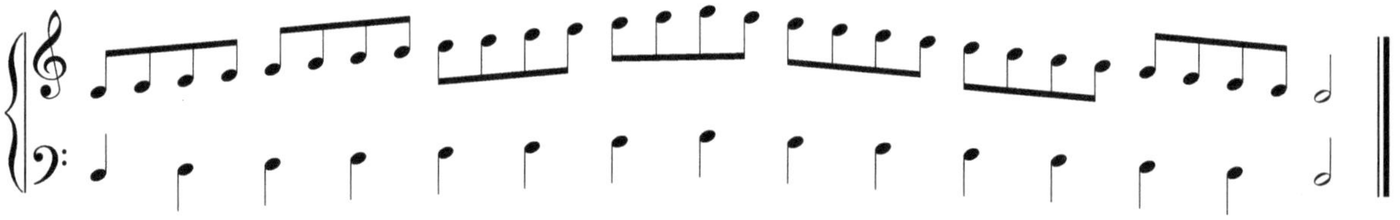

As for Twist 1, but reversed

Ratio Twist 3

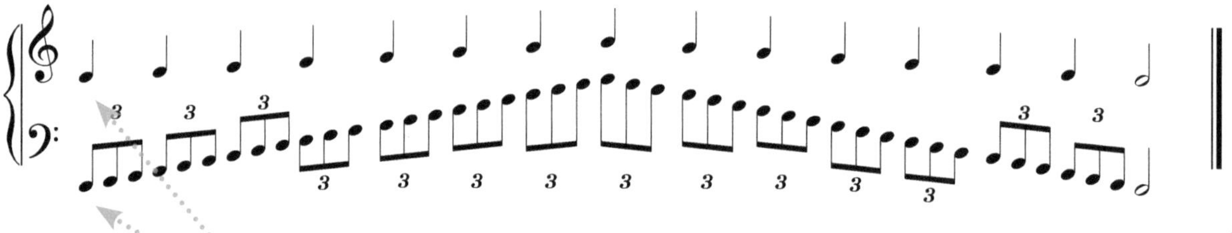

Space the hands at least 3 octaves apart at the start, or the Left hand will catch up with and run over the top of the Right hand!

Ratio Twist 4

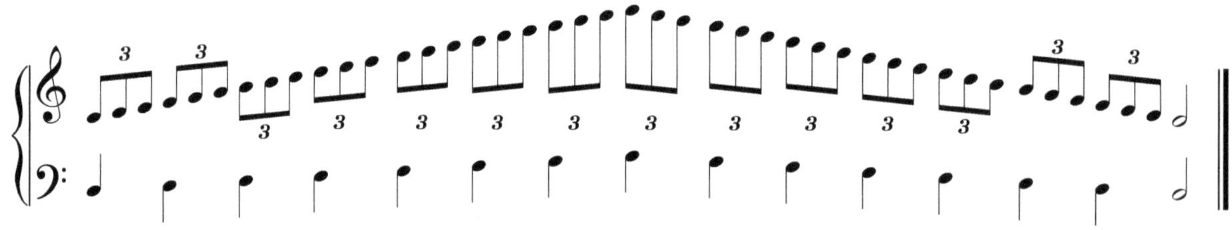

Twists: Ratio

Ratio Twist 5

LH rises 4 octaves here (!), start hands 4 octaves apart

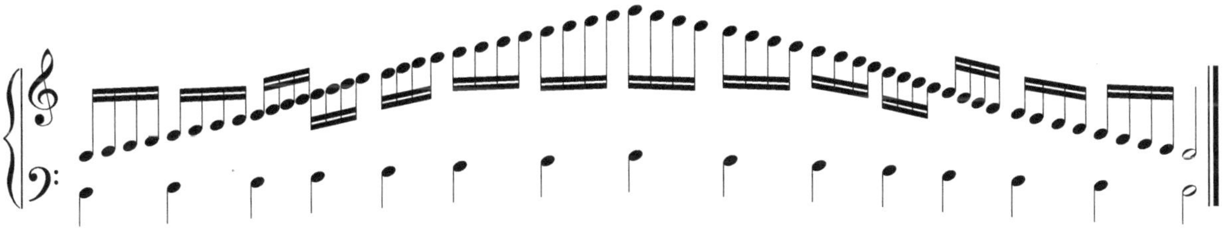

Ratio Twist 6

...start the RH low enough here to leave room for all 4 octaves

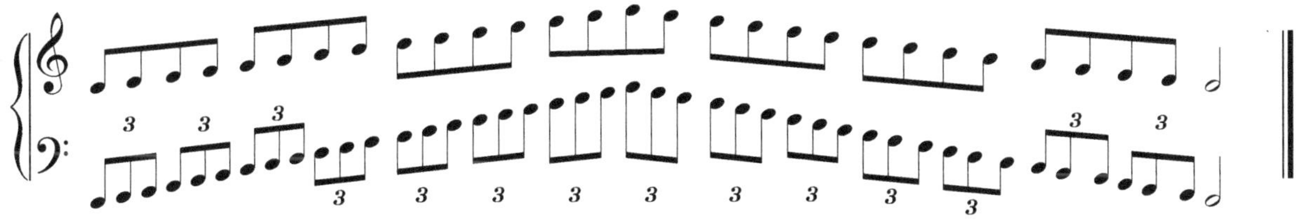

Ratio Twist 7

3 against 2!

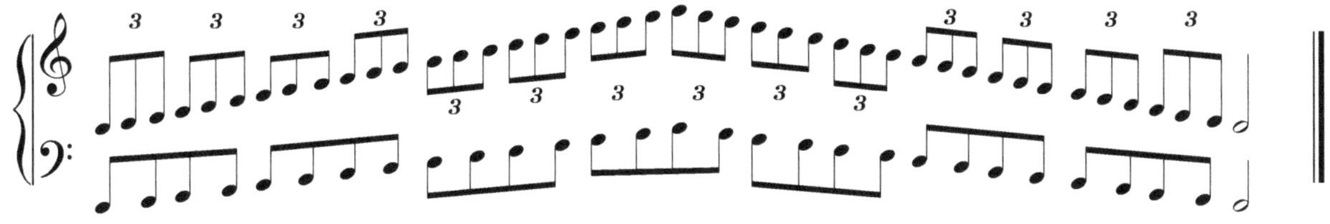

Ratio Twist 8

Bring out Right hand whenever you see ♩

Balance Twist 1

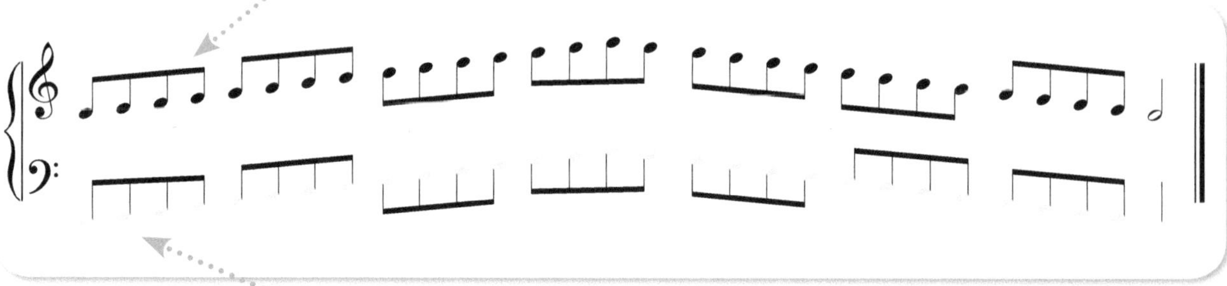

Keep Left hand quiet when notes are faded

Balance Twist 2

Like Twist 1, but reversed. Left hand is louder than right hand this time

Balance Twist 3

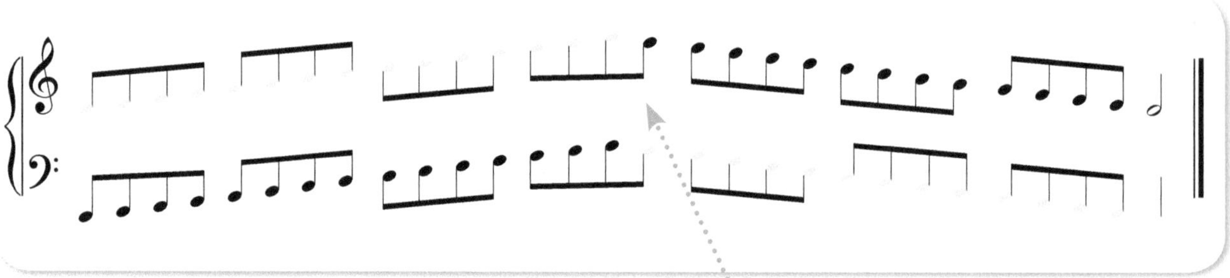

Don't be tricked—watch out for the swap half way through

Balance Twist 4

Twists: Balance

Balance twists require that you play one hand loudly while keeping the other hand quiet—just as you do when bringing out melodies

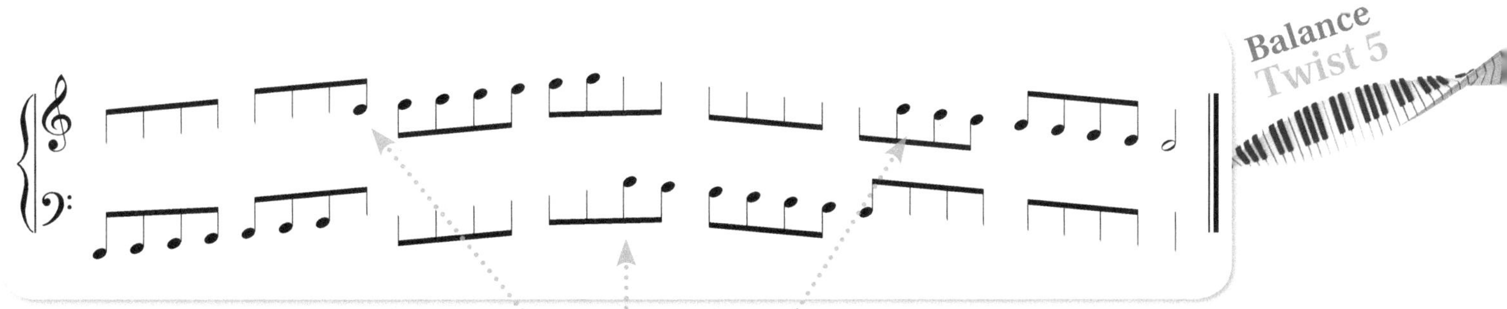

Swaps every octave!

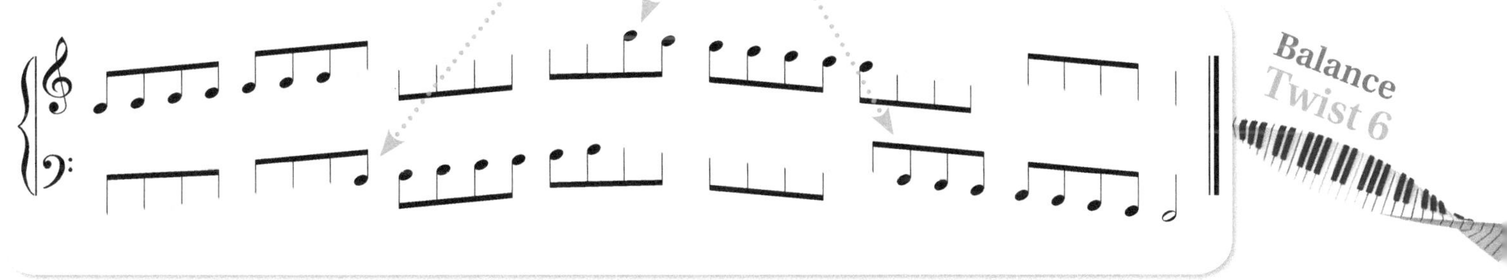

Both hands should be equally strong when both are shown as ♩

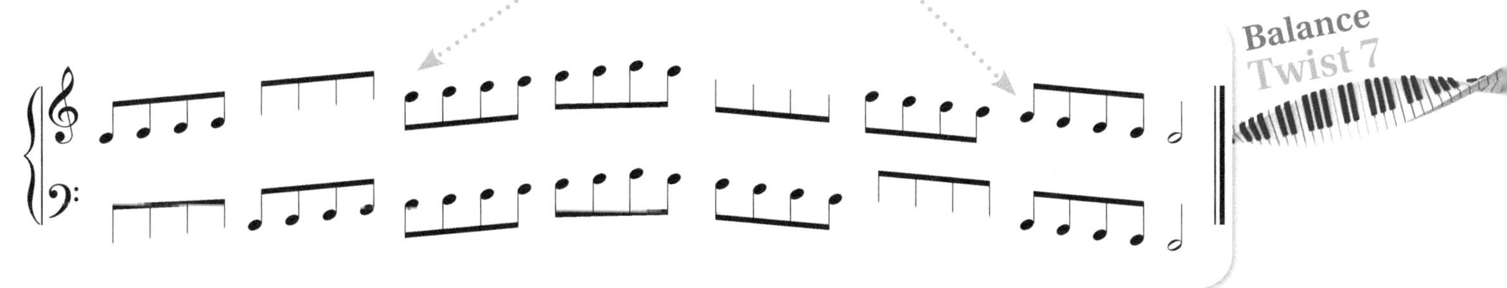

Good luck with this one...

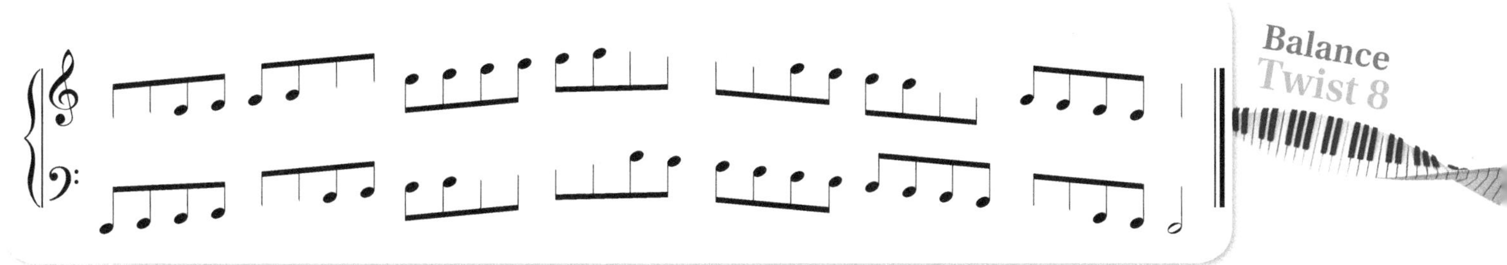

All Cacophony Twists are 2 octave scales

Cacophony Twist 1

RH plays the scale you're actually working on, while the LH...

...plays the major scale of the key starting a minor 3rd higher

So...if the Right hand is playing c minor, the Left hand will play Eb Major

Cacophony Twist 2

RH plays the scale you're actually working on, while the LH...

...plays the minor scale of the key starting a perfect 5th higher

So...if the Right hand is playing c minor, the Left hand will play g minor

Cacophony Twist 3

RH plays the scale you're actually working on, while the LH...

...plays the minor scale of the key starting a major 3rd lower

So if the Right hand is playing c minor, the Left hand would be playing Ab minor

Cacophony Twist 4

RH plays the scale you're actually working on, while the LH...

...plays the major scale of the key starting a semitone higher

Blech. These are named "cacophony twists" for a reason...

So...if the Right hand is playing c minor, Left hand would be playing F# minor

Cacophony Twist 5

RH plays the scale you're actually working on, while the LH...

...plays the minor scale of the key starting a tritone higher

Twists: Cacophony

These twists will have you playing one scale in one hand, and a completely different scale in the other(!)

Cacophony Twist 6

LH plays the scale you're actually working on, while the RH...

...plays the minor scale of the key starting a perfect 4th higher

Notice that on this page, the two hands have switched roles

Cacophony Twist 7

LH plays the scale you're actually working on, while the RH...

...plays the major scale of the key starting a major 3rd higher

So if the Left hand was playing c minor, the Right hand would play E Major

Cacophony Twist 8

LH plays the scale you're actually working on, while the RH...

...plays the major scale of the key starting a tone lower

More icky combinations that will have the neighbors complaining

Cacophony Twist 9

LH plays the scale you're actually working on, while the RH...

...plays the minor scale of the key starting a semitone lower

So if the Left hand was playing c minor, the Right hand would play F# Major(!)

Cacophony Twist 10

LH plays the scale you're actually working on, while the RH...

...plays the major scale of the key starting a tritone higher

...be careful to keep the ORIGINAL fingering for each note in the scale...

...so in C Major, the 2nd measure in the RH would use 231. 3rd measure would be 312

Cascade Twist 1

Cascade twists are mostly about THINKING...take time between measures

...this time, in C Major the 2nd measure RH would be 2312. Next would be 3123

Cascade Twist 2

The small notes simply mean "as fast as you can"...

Use the long notes to plan the next cascade... DON'T play on until you've pictured it correctly.

Cascade Twist 3

Twists: Cascade

These twists are shown in C Major—you'll need to apply the pattern to the scale you're actually doing.

Seriously, take all the time you need before the longer cascades—if you need several minutes to be able to picture the fingering properly, so be it!

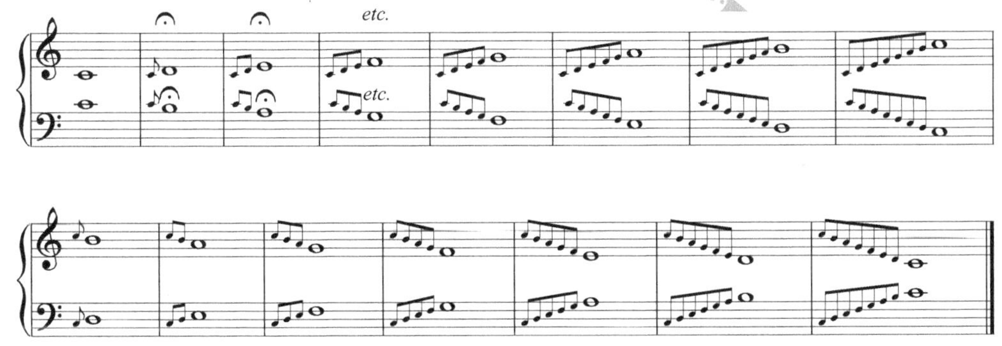

Cascade Twist 4

You might also want to do dummy runs of each new cascade on your piano lid before you try it for real

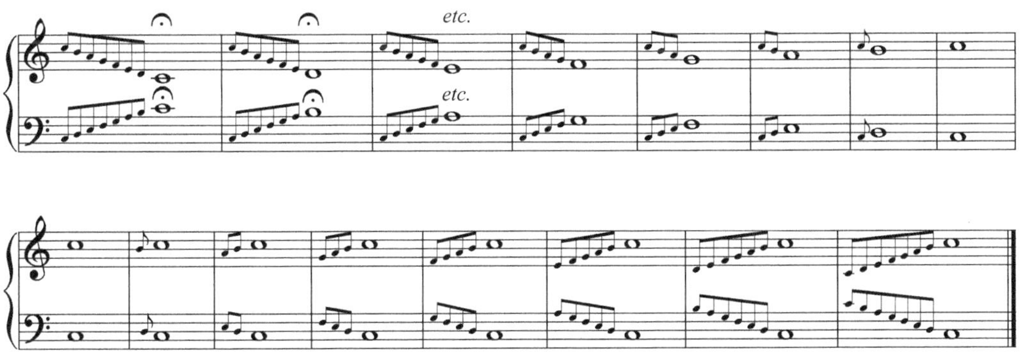

Cascade Twist 5

Don't forget...ORIGINAL fingering. So in C Major, the 2nd measure RH would be fingered 23123412

Cascade Twist 6

All Interval Twists are 2 octave scales

So if Right hand was playing C Major, Left hand starts on the E and plays 32132143 for its first octave

Interval Twist 1

Right hand starts on the tonic, Left hand a 6th below

So if Left hand was playing C Major, Right hand starts on the E and plays 31234123 for its first octave

Interval Twist 2

Left hand starts on the tonic, Right hand a 10th above

Fingered as in the previous example, except the RH is very close to the LH

Interval Twist 3

Left hand starts on the tonic, Right hand a 3rd above

Tricky because the hands are too far apart to easily see both hands at once.

Interval Twist 4

Both hands start on the tonic, but 4 octaves apart

So if Left hand was playing C Major, right hand starts on the A and plays 34123123 for its first octave.

Interval Twist 5

Left hand starts on the tonic, Right hand a 6th above.

Twists: Interval

Unlike the Cacophony Twists (p 84), both hands are playing the same scale, but one of the hands will be offset

Interval Twist 6

Right hand starts on the tonic, Left hand is a 3rd below.

So if RIght hand was playing C Major, Left hand starts on the A and plays 32143213 for its first octave

Interval Twist 7

Left hand starts on the tonic, Right hand a 4th above.

So if Left hand was playing C Major, Right hand starts on the F and plays 12341231 for its first octave

Interval Twist 8

Right hand starts on the tonic, Left hand a 7th below.

So if RIght hand was playing C Major, Left hand starts on the D below and plays 43213214 for its first octave

Interval Twist 9

Left hand starts on the tonic, Right hand a 9th above.

Just cruelly, horribly awkward—the hands get in the way of each other, and you can forget about legato

Interval Twist 10

Left hand starts on the tonic, Right hand a 2nd above.

Every measure in this twist actually takes exactly the same amount of time

Contrary Twist 1

One of the most well known scales twists of all time...

Contrary Twist 2

...and again, but everything turned upside down and back to front...

Contrary Twist 3

Twists: Contrary

These twists are shown in C Major—you'll need to apply the pattern to the scale you're actually doing

Good preparation for Cascade Twist 1, again targeting pairs of fingerings

Contrary Twist 4

Twist 4 extended into triplets...the quadruplet version of this twist is pretty much unplayable (try it)

Contrary Twist 5

As with all twists, be careful to always keep the original scales fingering throughout, even if it's less comfortable than an alternative

Contrary Twist 6

Bonus Achievements

Unexpected pedestals along the road to scales mastery

☐ Off and running
First Challenge completed for any scale

☐ Here's how it's done
All Very Easy scales promoted to Apprentice

☐ Speed Demon
First scale to earn all Tempo Milestone Challenges

☐ Annoy the neighbors
All Cacophony twists completed for all scales

☐ Le Grand Tour de diatonique
Grand Tour Challenge completed for all scales

☐ Nerves of steel
Marathon Tightrope completed for all scales

☐ Braille Scale
By feel alone Challenge completed for all scales

☐ Well Tempered Performances
Repertoire Challenge completed for all keys(!)

☐ Splatmaster Extreme
Splatmaster Challenge completed for all scales

☐ Beginner Breakthrough
First Beginner rank earned for any scale

☐ Apprentice Breakthrough
First Apprentice rank earned for any scale

☐ Skilled Breakthrough
First Skilled rank earned for any scale

☐ Master Breakthrough
First Master rank earned for any scale

☐ Legendary Breakthrough
First Legendary rank earned for any scale

☐ Yours-for-life Breakthrough
First Yours for life rank earned for any scale

☐ Very Easy Grandmaster
All Very Easy scales promoted to Grandmaster

☐ Easy Grandmaster
All Easy scales promoted to Grandmaster

☐ Moderate Grandmaster
All Moderate scales promoted to Grandmaster

- ☐ Challenging Grandmaster
  All Challenging scales promoted to Grandmaster
- ☐ Difficult Grandmaster
  All Difficult scales promoted to Grandmaster
- ☐ Not afraid of ghosts
  First scale with ghost notes promoted to Grandmaster
- ☐ Twisted and Turned
  First scale to complete all Twists
- ☐ Tenfold Beginner
  Beginner rank earned for any 10 scales
- ☐ Tenfold Apprentice
  Apprentice rank earned for any 10 scales
- ☐ Tenfold Skilled
  Skilled rank earned for any 10 scales
- ☐ Tenfold Master
  Master rank earned for any 10 scales
- ☐ Tenfold Legendary
  Legendary rank earned for any 10 scales
- ☐ Tenfold Yours-for-life
  Yours for life rank earned for any 10 scales
- ☐ Tin Challenge Milestone
  100 Challenges completed
- ☐ Bronze Challenge Milestone
  250 Challenges completed
- ☐ Silver Challenge Milestone
  500 Challenges completed
- ☐ Gold Challenge Milestone
  1,500 Challenges completed
- ☐ Platinum Challenge Milestone
  3,000(!) Challenges completed
- ☐ 24 Hour ScaleStorm
  30 Challenges completed in one day
- ☐ 7 Day ScaleStorm
  150 Challenges completed in one week
- ☐ Scales Immortal
  Yours for life earned for all scales(!)

Insane variety of practice quests

More than 1200(!) bite-sized practice quests to complete, as you take the piece from never-seen-it-before to concert ready. No two practice sessions will be identical.

Level up your piece

Just as you would in a computer game, Complete the quests, earn your Level ups, master the piece. It's complete preparation, one challenge at a time.

Disturbingly addictive

There's always just one more challenge to complete, one more Level within reach… Bootcamp practice is easy to start, hard to stop.

Uncompromisingly thorough

Random starting points, memorization drills, separate hand challenges … compared with what Bootcamp demands, the concert should be easy.

Brain crunching twists for mastery

The Bootcamp series is famous for its "twists"—devilishly difficult variations and challenges that stretch even the best prepared of students.

Look also for *Rhythm Bootcamp*

Transform your students' rhythm sightreading, one challenge at a time. Over 2,000 bite-sized rhythm reading quests to complete. Free audio files online, out now.

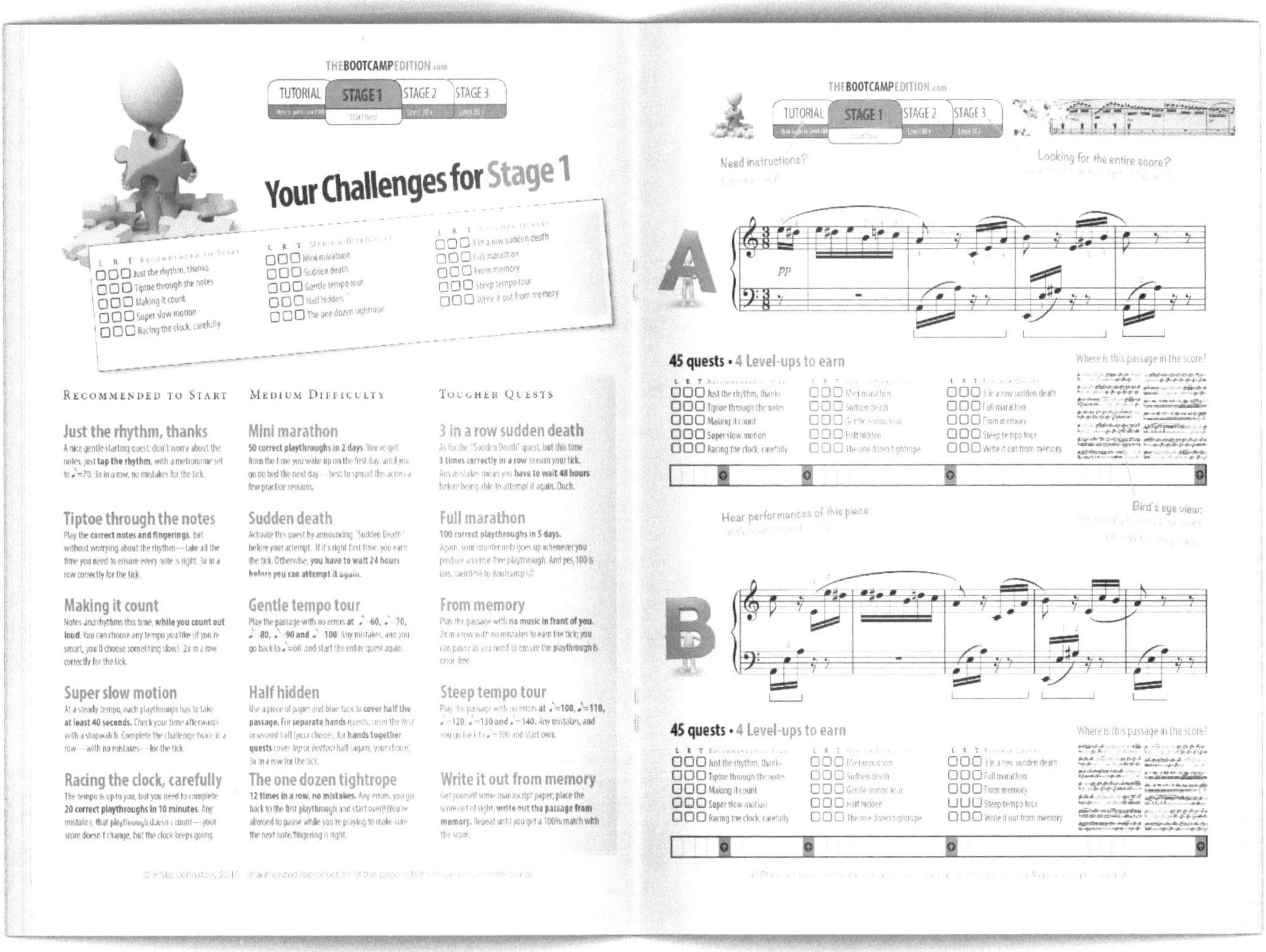

thebootcampedition.com

CPSIA information can be obtained
at www.ICGtesting.com
Printed in the USA
BVHW060002090721
611469BV00002B/12

* 9 7 8 0 9 5 8 1 9 0 5 4 1 *